The Right Way to Drown

A little art, a little faith, a little grief.

Aly Elliott

ISBN: 979-8-218-48530-6

For my parents; from Orchard Hill and Heaven, always cheering me on.

For my husband; my greatest asset, the love of my life.

For my beloved children; Boston, Keely, Callum, Beckham, Marnie, August. My reasons.

For Journalist Dave. Float on.

1

I stepped out of the hospital unprepared for the weather to do anything other than match my emotions. The light burned my eyes. *The audacity of the sun.* Around me, strangers were going about their day as usual. The earth kept spinning and the sun kept shining — but my child was dead. This wasn't the charming afternoon sun of my childhood. This wasn't the last time the daylight would sting either. I would continue to notice its intrusion. All the moments that lead me to that fateful day had failed to prepare me, even the ones that seemed like they should.

I was always comfortable talking about death. I saw enough Disney movies to consider the untimely deaths of people around me that I loved. I thought that was what everybody did as a child.

Now here I was, barely an adult by age and not an adult by preparedness, facing death from an unnatural angle. Nothing about this felt comfortable.

***

On Thursday morning, during my usual phone call with my mom, I told her that I didn't feel right. Something just felt *off*. Wrestling with my racing thoughts, I abbreviated my conversation with my mom, and called my doctor's office, who told me to come in. I loaded up my one-year-old son.

When did I last feel the baby move? Was it at dinner the night before? Maybe hours.

I couldn't remember and voiced my worry to my doctor, but she didn't seem terribly concerned. At 22 weeks pregnant, it was still pretty early for that — even though I'd been feeling movement for a while.

As we cruised into the doctor's office to the audible sounds of my heartbeat, Boston sat in his stroller cheerfully saying hello to everyone who walked by. He was probably looking for his Nana (my mom) or his daddy to stop in. We never went to a doctor's appointment without either my mom or husband, and sometimes both. He was a very busy toddler with dark blonde hair that we kept short with experimental haircuts in the kitchen. He liked to run his hands along a freshly buzzed noggin. He was the type of kid the leashes with backpacks attached were made for. I always kept a hand on him with the pinky wrapped around for an extra layer of protection.

I stacked a couple of tiny Tupperware containers on his stroller table to buy myself some focus in the waiting room. My nerves fluttered as they called me back into the room. The nurse who checked me in said that the doctor didn't want to waste time with a doppler to listen for a heartbeat and scare me since the baby was still relatively small, so she rolled a portable ultrasound machine into the room before even saying hello.

A beautiful little heartbeat at 145 beats per minute popped up on the screen, just as I completely expected. Despite my nervous energy, I had no reason to believe anything else might happen. As soon as I deeply exhaled with reassurance — the baby fluttered and kicked around. *Had I felt that before? Maybe I should have just waited a little while instead of coming in.*

Complete relief kept me from even thinking to ask to keep a printout from the ultrasound. At that point I was ready to get out of there so they could attend to the other patients. You know, those who had real issues — unlike me — who didn't even have an appointment. My doctor had squished this appointment in between regulars to ease my mind and I was so grateful.

All was well with the world. Boston, the wiggling baby in my belly, and I would be back here for my regular appointment on Monday— in just a few days. I called my husband, Sam, and then my mom to give them the update.

 To celebrate, Boston and I detoured to the park and spent the afternoon in the unusually warm, almost April sun.

Emboldened by my appreciation of the light, everything felt sun-drenched. The glimmer on the river next to the park to the dew that dripped from the bottom of the slide was bright. My son's boisterous giggle echoed in my grateful heart that afternoon.

✳✳✳

The following Monday felt like the heat of summer had already hit the Midwest — challenging my wardrobe. It was the second day of April and I had managed my entire first pregnancy to avoid wearing actual maternity clothes. Thanks to empire waistlines and low-rise jeans being fashionable for the day — my pregnant belly sat right between those two styles as it grew.

"Well, this is new." My doctor chuckled as she motioned towards the rubber bands I had looped through my jeans and the buttonhole — allowing a little more space. We laughed about only making it this far before a new wardrobe was necessary this time.

"Maybe this little one isn't so little after all!" She continued as flashes of a new chubby cheeked baby reeled through my mind.

I thought back to my firstborn's round cheeks and pile of hair right at the top of his head. I remembered how he hated his car seat and offered his first giggles to the dog. Once you have your first baby, it's hard to picture having one any different than that first.

I tried to imagine a new baby being different in some way than the one I already had. *Maybe a lighter blonde? Maybe one of those babies you hear about who like to be driven around the neighborhood to go to sleep?* I couldn't imagine it, and babies have a way of surprising us every time.

My mom was in town for this appointment so we had plans to head to the mall for lunch and shopping right around noon, when I should be finished at the doctor —rigged jeans and all. She and Boston were in the little playroom down the hall from the exam rooms and around the corner from the ultrasound room. Occasionally, I'd hear an excited giggle from him as he was getting spoiled by his Nana.

This was the last appointment before the big gender reveal. This was long before cakes were baked with pink or blue or elaborate videos were made to announce boy or girl. Our gender reveal would be in the ultrasound room at the doctor's office, and both Mom and my husband would come along to this appointment.

Boston would get to see "his" baby, that I just knew was a boy. My biggest concern was whether the baby would cooperate enough to see girl or boy on ultrasound. Knowing that appointment was next, I expected this one to be short and ordinary — especially since I had gotten an extra peek at the baby just a few days before.

As we were wrapping up the usual doctor-patient banter, she pulled out the doppler, and immediately found that sweet sound of a heartbeat. I noticed she lingered on it longer than usual though. *What was the problem?* I could hear the heartbeat — it sounded fine to me. But something kept me from asking. The laughter that had filled the room a moment before was gone. I could suddenly hear the clock on the wall. *Tick. Tick. Tick.* I became very aware of my own breathing. *Inhale. Exhale.* I studied her face and saw her lips moving as she stared at her watch. She was counting each beat.

I finally managed to ask her, "Is everything okay?" *What was she hearing that I wasn't.*

"I hear a heartbeat." *Yeah, me too.*

"But it's very slow." *Oh.*

119, I read on the screen of the doppler. *Why was she concerned about that? It didn't seem slow to me.* None of the pregnancy books would think twice about it. I had read them all, cover to cover.

91, She whispered the second number under her breath right before she abruptly left the room. I was feeling the baby move during the appointment. I heard the heartbeat. Slower heartrate just meant a boy. Right?

Right?

She was gone only a matter of seconds when she popped her head back in and waved for me to follow her down to the ultrasound room. My mind raced as we walked down the hallway. I could hear my mom and son in the room at the corner — I was glad they wouldn't know I was right there. Boston would reach for me and maybe cry. Then I might. He would be crying to be held, but I would be overcome with worry. *Let's just get this ultrasound done. Just like last week.*

I was worried I'd find out the sex of the baby and Sam wouldn't be here. For a moment, I thought of fun ways to tell him. I could get a little outfit for the boy or girl (probably boy) and have it sitting out when he got home from work that night or I could have Boston tell him. Maybe we could even go straight to his work, so neither of us would have to wait. Would I be able to keep a secret long enough to tell him in a cute way? Probably not. I also couldn't wait to find out myself. I didn't even have time to send him a text to let him know what was happening —everyone and everything around me was moving too quickly.

As I laid back on the ultrasound chair, my hands were shaking. The jelly was warmer for the ultrasound than the doppler jelly had been, and the skin on my stomach was still sticky from when the doctor had been slowly counting each beat. I was surprised when the door opened, and the room got dark — my doctor appeared. She had never been in the room for an ultrasound. Saying nothing, she turned to the screen on the wall in front of me.

Something was off. The baby was curled up and the heartbeat was… heavier than it had seemed before. The three of us; the ultrasound tech, the doctor, and myself watched it silently. It seemed like forever. 92 beats at first. *That's better than it was a moment ago.*

A quick glance at the other women in the room and my flicker of hope was fleeting. Neither turned towards me, or said a word. I turned my attention back to my baby that was still on the screen. The time between each beat got longer and longer. The bright line was the only light in the room as it flickered towards the top of the bar and back down again. The sound was muffled.

82 beats per minute.
68 beats per minute.
52. 38.

As it fell into the 20s, the ultrasound tech pulled the wand off my skin. My voice cracked as I begged her to put it back. She listened.

By the time the wand was back on my stomach, there was no heartbeat to find. The doctor said nothing and stepped out of the room.

"I'm so sorry." the tech whispered.

I could hear my own heartbeat in my throat. It was at that moment that I felt as if I were watching myself playing a role on evening television, where everything moves in slow motion, and everyone works with desperation to save a life.

I wanted a big, dramatic rescue attempt. I wanted other people to panic alongside me.

NO …..I wanted to scream, but only managed barely a whisper. *Please.* My mind couldn't understand why there wasn't more commotion. *Someone, do something.* I begged her to shock me.

"Oh no, we can't. It wouldn't…." She trailed off and now it was her voice that was cracking.

"I'm so sorry." she whispered again.

The doctor came back in, her eyes red and makeup newly off now.

"Are you here alone?" I shook my head.

My mom and son were in the room down the hall playing Legos —blissfully unaware what had just happened. I considered for a second how they had no idea how everything just changed

"Do you want to tell them?" The doctor asked me. Just as the words left her lips, the tears started. My hands trembled as I struggled to speak. Suddenly, it felt too loud in that room. It was all I could do to cover my face and shake my head once again.

Not long after, my mom's shadow appeared in the doorframe. I couldn't see her face at first, until my eyes resolved with the new light streaming in. The room was still dark, but the image of my dying baby was no longer on the screen. My mother held Boston in her arms.

Normally, Boston would reach for me immediately. This time, he didn't. Instead, he clung to his Nana with both fists on her shirt collar. Maybe he was scared because I was scared, and he could sense it. Maybe it was the dark and he couldn't quite see me. Maybe my fear and shock reverberated through the walls of the ultrasound room. With the light of the hallway behind him, his eyes searched the dark room, and he quietly tucked his head into her neck.

As my eyes focused towards the bright hallway, I saw the tears rolling down my mother's face. She was always strong when we needed her to be, but on that day, we needed to call on the strength only God could provide. Strength for the room to stop spinning. Strength for every second to not be a struggle to breathe. Strength for every word that would leave our lips. Strength for every phone call we needed to make. Strength to leave that dark room.

"Do I need to leave the room?" I asked the ultrasound technician. It felt like business had to be taken care of. Things needed to happen. I needed some chaos. I needed some distraction. I needed to move. I needed anything to pretend what was happening —wasn't.

I looked at the "please turn phones off" sign in front of me, but I didn't want to leave the room. It was too bright out there. There were too many people out there. I handed my cell phone to my mom. "Please call Sam." Every word from my mouth was saturated with desperation. She bit her lip and took my phone to give her son-in-law the worst news any father could get. I flipped the phone open and scrolled down to his name. With it still open and its light filling up that small room, I handed it to my mom.

She returned mere seconds later, her face strained and drawn. Her expression was one I'd never seen before- a deep sadness.

"I'm so sorry. I just can't." The words squeaked out of her mouth. She literally, physically could not do it.

I looked at the tech and motioned towards the sign that seemed far too cheerful now. "Oh, it's fine. You're fine." She said, seemingly relieved there was something easy to answer.

She handed my open phone back to me and I did what I knew I should have been doing anyway. When I heard the comforting voice of my completely confused husband on the other line, I barely got words out as the tears flowed freely.

"The baby died. The baby is gone." I said to him, in complete chaos, almost shouting. There was no other way they were coming out. Time stood still, and yet it seemed like the very next moment he was by my side.

***

I met my husband in my first class on my first day of college. He was the clean-cut kid in a class of first year art students trying to display creativity through blonde dreadlocks and painted jeans. His hair was buzz cut and face was handsome. He wore button down shirts and sweaters when most everyone else wore the same thing from the day before. He was a little obnoxious and I was too quiet for him, but we fell into the same friend group anyway.

My mom had taken my picture before I left for school every first day since kindergarten, and the first day of college was no different. I was the baby of the family and every first day picture for me was a last for my mom's children. I felt like I was pretending to be a grown-up and so was everybody else there. My mom reminded me more than once to "look friendly". I think she was afraid I'd never make friends or get married because of my unfriendly face. God Himself would have to handle my introductions as I preferred to observe for a while.

As I drove the 20 minutes to campus on the first day of class, I ignored my shaking hands. I turned Bob Dylan's voice up in my car's CD player and knew I could reach Mom at any time on my giant brick of a Nokia cell phone with a broken case.

When I'm nervous, I tend to put on a face of irritation, to put it nicely. It's the same face my cat gets around loud children, and we call her "flat eared kitty". It's not the face that says I'm here to make friends. And I wasn't there to make friends. I have never really been one to lean on friends. I had secure roots at home and didn't feel a void that made friends feel necessary. I was open to it, but not desperate for it. I was there for all business. I had moved on from my days of dressing like Jackie Kennedy and made her daughter-in-law, Carolyn Bessett Kennedy my style icon for the last few years of high school and into college. My unofficial uniform was all black fitted, simple clothes and my blonde hair slicked back into a low ponytail or bun. my unofficial uniform.

My first class was Drawing I. I was the third person in the room. I could hear my oldest sister's voice in my head calling me a nerd for arriving so early. I triple checked that I was in the right place and hoped no one would talk to me before class started. Small talk always ends up about the weather and I don't care nearly as much about the weather as I end up talking about it. I'm a midwestern girl; I'll take a foot of snow or a heat advisory and anything in between. But I don't need to talk about it.

I scanned each student as they walked in the room. A split-second judgement was made and then it became a matter of waiting to see if I had been right. Two boys caught my attention that day. They caught everyone's attention because they were loud and fast friends. Sam was one of them — he seemed arrogant. Dan was the other, he was the hippy that became a friend to everyone. I was perfectly content to just quietly observe, unfriendly face and all.

Each time we tacked our completed projects onto the wall, we had to choose one to critique. What happened often was that whoever had to go first chose a friend's drawing. They'd sandwich a sugarcoated critique in between all the things they loved about it. Not very conducive to growth, but easier to stomach in front of everyone else. I was guilty of this myself most of the time. If someone had been rude or annoying, it was easier to give them brutal honesty.

Sam was always honest. Always. So honest, in fact, people would visibly cringe if he chose their drawing to critique. It wasn't going to be sugarcoated and it wasn't going to be sandwiched in between compliments. It may not have any redeeming qualities and he wasn't afraid to say so. I braced myself each time, but he never chose my work.

***

We were still in the ultrasound room when he arrived at the hospital. He was as handsome as the day we met, and I didn't even find him obnoxious anymore. The clean-cut art kid was now seven years older, and we'd been married four years. His arms and chest were covered in ink that told the stories of our lives, and his still-young face was covered in a heavy five o'clock shadow.

He'd been hanging signs for work and left a stop sign hanging upside down as soon as he received the call. It would hang upside down the whole week until he went back to fix it. Even after it was fixed, it would forever remind me of the worst moment of our lives.

When it was time to leave the dark of the ultrasound room, I grabbed my husband's arm. I had been in that room for what felt like years. He had only been there minutes. He hadn't had time to process it all. He was holding Boston and together they were looking at the image of our baby that had been printed out in shiny black and white. There was our baby all curled up… still. *Still.* When I touched his arm, I was overwhelmed with gratitude for the strength he was showing —physical and emotional — both palpable. I thought he didn't know it was time to go, but it wasn't for him yet. He wasn't ready to leave that room and face the light of the hallway.

The obnoxious sun doubled my vision as we left the hospital. I felt like I was drowning in the sunlight. I felt like I was drowning in general. The entire world was out there, just going on about their lives, meanwhile my baby had just died.

The next few hours were full of phone calls. My sisters had been carrying on very normal, very sunny days when I called them. One was on the playground of the school she taught at. I pictured her out in the sun with the children running and laughing around her. I pictured how the words I would repeat a thousand times that day brought clouds no one else could see. My other sister was at the park with her children. Again, with the sun. Again, with the clouds. I answered the same questions. I asked myself the same things. I fumbled around the answers, they fumbled around for more to say.

What else is there to say?

My baby is dead. The baby I carried for 22 weeks and 3 days, the baby being knit in my womb with intricate detail, the baby I prayed for, the baby that was just wiggling all around with a strong heartbeat days before, was dead. *It may have been sunny that day- but it was one of the darkest of my life.*

2

My mom usually left early enough to make it home before dark when she visited us, but today was different. No time seemed like the right time to leave me. But as the sun dipped out of view, she couldn't delay any longer. Before she left, she and Sam discussed how to care for me. She asked if he'd make sure I eat, and what she could do to help us rest. Should she give Boston a bath before she went home? *No. His splashing was a beautiful distraction, no matter how fleeting.*

Maybe a better woman would've insisted she didn't need care —but not me. I did. I needed what they couldn't give me. They needed what my body was supposed to carry, and failed. I failed. My body was supposed to do what women's bodies had done since the beginning of time — but it didn't.

I remember so many random moments from the day our baby's heartbeat stopped. I curled my knees into the back cushions of the couch, looking through the picture window next to it. I could see far up through the bare branches of the sycamore tree, to the sky. I felt like I'd remember every second of that day in desperate detail, to hold tight to the only memories I could of my baby. In the fury of significance that every little moment took on in those hours before, I felt so grateful that I got to watch the heartbeat slow. If it had to stop, I wanted to know. That gut-wrenching moment — as broken as it left me — was a gift.

To make sure I was eating, Sam made pasta that night. It was one of the meals that was born out of a pregnancy craving and quickly became a family favorite. He placed the familiar plates in front of us, and they both went untouched. Boston played in his highchair as usual, picking up elbow macaroni with both hands. He ate most of them, smeared some into the plastic tray, and slid some off the edges.

Staring at that plate of full pasta, I remembered the summer when I was eight years old. There was a tornado in the town between my hometown and the mall we shopped at, about an hour away. We had plans for the next day and didn't realize the extent of the damage in the days before the internet. We drove slowly down the highway that doubled as the main street of that little town that had been devastated.

There was a diner on the left side of the road. 24 hours before, it had consisted of a bustling staff, filled tables, multiple conversations. Now, as we drove by slowly through the debris in the road, only two walls remained. The back wall stood, where several people's lives had been saved by a quick-thinking manager who put every customer and staff member in the walk-in freezer.

What I remember most is that despite the roof and half the building being gone — the food was still on the tables. The booths lined up just as they always had. The plates on the tables were as if they had just been served. That image burned into my mind, and I only thought of it occasionally, usually during a bad storm. The storm that left our pasta untouched that evening was a storm of a different kind.

Boston ate his "noonles" as well as he ever did. He threw some overboard to our dog below and she let it hit her in the face and bounce off. She wasn't there for people food; she was there for us. Our Mimi dog just knew.

Whenever I crawled onto the couch waiting to snuggle our 1-year-old that was too busy to be snuggled, as usual, our

Mimi dog snuggled like a champ. She was a white Australian Shepherd with black spots and blue eyes. Her fluffy fur comforted me from her favorite place — the top of the couch by the front window.

Even though she was probably a little too big for the spot she chose, she hoisted herself onto the cushions that then squished down to half their size. From that perch, she could watch for intruders and, rather than defend our home, be the first to clear out. She did what we needed her to do — eat popcorn and snuggle and let us all pet her endlessly. She had been our practice baby before Boston was born and had taken the brunt of the learning curve. She was the one we had to consider when we were going somewhere. We had to know she was taken care of. We had to feed her and love on her and receive that love in return.

That night we all stayed in the little living room on Fairlawn Avenue in a little brick house that was just exactly the comfort we needed. We kept the television on until it was just music videos and infomercials. I was relieved for it to be anything other than babies. My eyes felt heavy but couldn't find rest. As my body sunk deeper into the cushions and my head weighted down the pillow, my mind was too busy to allow my eyes to close.

We went back to the hospital the next day to check again — maybe it was a mistake. Maybe the doctor and nurses told us we could come back again just so we' d leave the day before. Maybe if we just stayed in that dark ultrasound room, we could avoid a reality we weren't ready to face. I told God countless times that night that I wouldn't even question it. If the baby were alive — we'd just be grateful — be better people. We wouldn't need answers or be mad at the technician — nothing bad at all. I'd do anything for it to be a mistake.

"Let this be a nightmare, now let me wake up. *Please.*"

My bargaining with God went unanswered in the very specific way I prayed. The next morning, the baby was in the very same position we had seen the day before. This time, though, the room was filled with people. People that wanted to help and couldn't. People that tried to say the right thing and didn't. Family members who wanted to be there but weren't sure why.

The next few days were a flurry. At some point early on, it was as if I was beside myself. I became a ghost walking next to my body, letting it work through things that had to get done. I couldn't do it myself, so my mom and her mother were there every single day. My grandmother's sister raised my mom and was who I considered my grandmother. I hadn't spent a lot of time with the woman who birthed my mom but didn't raise her before this. My grandmother died when I was nine and I felt like I needed one now, so we found ourselves in a new relationship.

During those first few weeks after losing the baby, my mom and I went to Macy's department store almost every day. I was afraid to stop doing things because if I waited too long, every trip would be a "this is the first time since" milestone, so we'd find an excuse to go. I had enough milestones.

So, we powered through the mall like we were born for it. We cried when we needed to and tried to find a laugh, but there were none. We picked out clothes for the funeral. I couldn't try them on because my belly was still full from pregnancy, so we just had to guess. I probably didn't need to get shoes for the funeral because they would forever be my "funeral shoes", but I did anyway.

On one trip, my mom bought me a necklace with little white diamonds in a circle and a blue sapphire inside. I thought it looked like a belly with a baby inside it. Everything in my life; the little things and the big things became a mark of whether they happened before or after. I think about this often.

Right now, as I write this or as you read this, someone somewhere is having the worst moment of their life — it's happening. This date and time will be engrained into someone's memory as the pivotal instant that split their life into before and after. It was many years later and many pivotal moments later that I realized we aren't limited to only one. Unfortunately.

Rather than the first trips out becoming milestones, Macy's became my grief store. Every time I see the sign or step foot in one, I think back to when my mother and I tried to evade grief. Or at least slow it down.

Somewhere along the blur of days we couldn't stop crying and nights we couldn't sleep — Sam and I decided to wait to deliver our baby. Part of me just wanted to hold the baby a little longer and not believe any of it was real. Part of me was still walking beside my real self, waiting to be whole again. Part of me was still bargaining with God. I was holding out hope that there had been a mistake. Not logical hope, but *hope*.

Miracles happen every day, I told myself. And they do, but not because we beg for them. We may not even notice them. Each intricate detail woven into the fiber of babies being formed in the womb, the rising and falling of each ocean tide, how anybody finds *that* person that gets them in a sea of people — all miracles. Seeds sprouting into trees, offering oxygen and shade — miracle. Each rise and fall of my son's chest, with his lips taking in and letting go of air is a miracle. I counted them every night that week.

Easter was the Sunday after that fateful 11:00 am appointment and we didn't want to ruin the holiday for everyone. As it turns out, we were probably doing that anyway, but it was a good excuse to buy some time just still being pregnant. A dark cloud hung over that Easter Sunday both literally and figuratively. It was cold and cloudy, and we went through the motions under the notion that we wanted Boston to have his Easter. We wanted him to carry his too-big basket, search for the bunny, and find all the colored plastic eggs his little hands could carry. I tried not to let my mind drift to the basket in the closet that we had gotten weeks before — a basket that would remain empty now.

The days passed us by in a blur of tears and sadness, visitors, flowers, and cards. Sam and I split our time between inconsolable sadness and out of body experiences. We went to church with my mom and dad to the little country church, an unassuming cinderblock building painted white, where I was baptized. A girl I had known since we were toddlers came up to me after services. The two of us had played soccer together most of our lives, and swam together most summer days.

We'd known each other well, but she was a quiet person and not overly talkative. I had almost made it to the car without eye contact from anyone. I don't know, exactly, what I was avoiding by not speaking. Maybe I didn't want to cry in front of people anymore. Maybe I was tired of the looks of pity. Maybe I felt guilty for not doing the first job I was supposed to do as a mother to this baby. Maybe I was tired of facing other people's sorrow and figuring out what to say back. Maybe I just didn't have a reason.

Being from a small town and tiny childhood church, I was certain everyone knew that our baby died. I imagined they had announced it at the end of services to a light gasp of sadness. I was relieved I didn't have to say it. For once, the small-town circuit of knowing everyone else's business offered a little relief.

I turned to my longtime friend on that sunny Sunday and looked at her with what was probably a very blank expression on my face.

"Aly, I'm so sorry." she whispered to me.

I nodded. Nothing was the right thing to say at that time. Everything made me mad. But this? This was exactly right. No explanation. No "but." No "everything happens for a reason." Just sorrow. She was the hand on my back at just the right time. Teammates forever, as it turns out.

It was exactly what I needed, but I don't recall if I told her that. I gave her a hug and we both turned away from each other. I sat in the car waiting for my husband to buckle our son into the seat and let the tears silently glide down my face under my sunglasses. I was safe from eye contact now. And those families I had known my entire life were safe from eye contact with me, safe from not knowing what to say, and safe from asking any questions. They could return to their normal Sundays, having brunch at the diner down the road, or going back home to cook a late lunch.

There were many instances like that in the coming days and weeks. I felt like I was wearing my story all over my face, but now I realize nobody else had any idea. There really were no "right" words. How right they felt depended on who was saying them and my mindset at that exact moment.

Even the right words were wrong because how could anything be "right," then?

As the time got closer to the date our baby would be born, the days blurred together more. I spent my time making lists. I've heard that a person's habits are exaggerated in grief, and lists were mine. I needed to know that every detail was covered. We had so little time. I kept telling myself this was the only thing we'd be able to do to parent this baby and it needed to be perfect. Every little detail.

We traveled back and forth from our home to my hometown to prepare. Our baby would be laid to rest next to my grandmother, in the cemetery I'd been caretaker of as a little girl, as a teenager, and every Memorial Day and Christmas as a grown woman.

***

I was spoiled growing up. I know that. I would not call myself a spoiled brat, though my older sisters might tell you otherwise. There was no shortage of love, attention, and support in our family. I grew up having a beautiful yellow gingham canopy bed as my own, in a room with farm animals all over the wall. After I decorated that yellow gingham with permanent black marker shortly after I got it, my mother told me I was going to keep it forever.

My room was situated between my two older sisters' rooms, so you had to walk through mine to get to my middle sister's room. That was where we'd have stereo wars on school mornings and my room would end up the octagon if one sister thought the other had stolen her sweater (obviously, I was never involved in that. I was born an old soul, but I also was five and eight years younger than them, so the sizes were off).

22

Our room situation made for an easy transition if one of us had a bad dream and needed a sister in the middle of the night the way my middle sister and I sometimes did. If we begged enough and cried to Mom, our oldest sister would let us sleep on her floor Christmas Eve. Like a dog, you may be thinking. Yes, and we were thrilled.

I had a nightlight in the window of my bedroom that looked like balloons. If my nightlight didn't go on at night, we'd get a call from my grandmother to make sure all was well because she could see it from her house. Our little cape cod style house on the top of Orchard Hill was built on the same property as my grandparents' house. We knew their house as Pleasant Ridge. That reminds me, I should probably name our home now so my kids have an idyllic description rather than solely memories of my lamenting about how close our neighbors are. My mom grew up on Pleasant Ridge; she told stories and wrote poems of making the hike up Orchard Hill with her favorite cousin to play. It made sense that she'd make a home there with my dad.

Summers were spent in the swimming pool at my grandparents' house and catching fireflies in the yard. We'd march down the driveway in our jelly shoes early in the day when the air still felt cold. The smell of bacon and coffee greeted us on the back porch as we said our good mornings. We were surrounded by cousins, aunts, uncles, cousins that seemed more like aunts, friends from church, and some aunts that were actually aunts but raised like cousins. Maybe we gave Facebook the idea for "it's complicated". Let's just say there were a lot of people. We'd end our elder aunt's morning exercise sessions in the pool with a cannonball and squeal. We'd pretend to be Olympic gymnasts doing flips across the shallow end and Superman as we'd fly across the bottom of the pool that resembled the tops of buildings.

Someone's mom would force us out long enough to eat and rest before another cannonball parade off the diving board with freshly applied sunscreen. Our hair never quite dried before we'd jump back in the water. We had to clear out of the pool at dusk because the bats and birds would swoop down to dine on the bugs dappling the water's edge. Nobody wanted to be a part of that, but my Gramps sure found it funny.

Damp hair and slight sunburn kept the evening air feeling chilly, so we'd run for the fireflies; partly catching them, partly just batting them around. The cousins all ended the summer evening on the edge of the hill, pumping our fists in the air, hopeful that the teenagers cruising by would honk at us. My oldest sister would hope no one would recognize her family.

I had the exhilarating joy of enjoying hundreds of family members for lunches and play and then I had the escape of a quiet house with just my family less than a mile away. See, I told you I was spoiled.

My grandmother spread love around almost completely equally. She loved everybody like they were her favorite, but her real favorite was always the baby. And that happened to be me. My grandpa was less diplomatic, and I was just his plain old favorite. He never outright said that, but we were very close.

One summer morning when I was 11, I was getting ready for my usual morning swim at my grandparents' house, my mom said someone was on the phone for me. Hmm, that wasn't usual at all. The summer sun was still pretty low, and I knew the pool water would still be chilly. My friends and I didn't usually make plans until much later in the day. We were far too young to drive, but old enough to time asking our parents just right. Must be big news!

It was big news, but not the kind my mind went to first. I thought maybe a trip to the amusement park or a sleepover. Instead, I heard from my best friend and fellow 11-year-old that two of our friends were in a car accident and one of the girls had died.

Suddenly, she felt like she'd been my best friend. I thought back to the Halloween party she had the year before. I was dressed like a 1950s girl with a poodle skirt and a varsity letter sweater. With my hair in a ponytail and rippling bow, we all danced to the monster mash. I thought about how she scratched at the bug bites on her arms and left big marks. I thought about how her dark hair was so curly and I was a little jealous because my in-between hair was sometimes curly, sometimes straight, and mostly in-between. I thought about how our desks had been pushed up next to each other in class, both a part of four desks with an "antarctica" sign above it.

A few days later, we read her obituary in the paper. The last name was different than the one I knew. It talked about her family and her hobbies. I hadn't really known that either. But I had pictures of her from a field trip to see tractors, and memories from the Halloween party. I had antarctica and that was all I'd have. I knew how this all worked now.

My oldest sister let me wear one of her old outfits for the funeral. I thought it was so grown up, but it was a black pinafore with a white silk shirt underneath. I wore my half curly hair down in memory of my very curly-haired friend.

Somehow, I convinced my mom I should go with my best friend, her mom, and another friend from their neighborhood. It probably didn't take much convincing because my mother was not one keen to show up at a funeral as an extra. What neither of us knew was that my friend's mother was going to drop us off at the door.

So three of us 11- year-olds arrive at our friend's funeral. Though growth spurts had started, we all seemed very small in that room. We each signed our names in large letters on the guest sheet. I wasn't sure her mom would remember who I was. We looked around from the back row of chairs, taking in various family members with bandages and braces from the accident. Her mother's boyfriend had been driving, but it wasn't his fault. All the news and my mom and dad said so. He stood at the front by the open casket, his nose in a bandage. It was hard to not look at him, but I didn't want to make eye contact.

After what seemed like a million years and a lot of convincing between the three of us that the other should be first, we all walked up to the front together. I had been to funerals before, but never without my parents, my landing place, my cover. This time, it was time to grow up — fast.

I felt the old ladies staring at us. I felt her mother's eyes turn to us. We stood by the foot of the casket and looked at our friend. She looked the same; *exactly the same.* She had the same scratches on her arms from bug bites, same curly dark hair. I had never seen her sleeping, but it probably looked just like this. Her hands resting on her belly looked like they were raising and lowering with breath, ever so slightly. They weren't, of course, and I reminded myself of that, but I sure felt like I could see it.

How long did we need to stand there? What was expected of us? Were we supposed to talk to her? Talk to her mother's boyfriend? Say she looks pretty? Say we're sorry? I wanted to do what a grown up would do.

I felt like I should cry. I knew that's what people do at funerals, and it came easily at my grandmother's. I wished it hadn't. Now I wished for a tear to drip out because it would seem more authentic. But the pressure to cry was more than my pre-teen emotions could handle.

Her mom patted my shoulder, and I counted the seconds down until it felt like we could appropriately leave. In that room full of people in shock from burying a child; their daughter, sister, niece, cousin, best friend, granddaughter — I suddenly felt like I hadn't known her that well at all. I felt like an intruder in their private moment, and I was ready to go home.

We waited on the sidewalk for my best friend's mother to pick us up and none of us said a word in the car. Once I got home, in my Precious Moments journal, I wrote a poem trying to make sense of it all and scratched it out. Words failed me that day.

3

Here I was, 14 years later, and I still didn't feel grown up. I wondered if my mom should call the funeral home because it seemed like something a grown up would do and I had never really felt grown up. *Not yet.*

My 1-year-old played in the sun-filled playroom, batting a plastic golf ball from one side to the next and around Mimi, our dog. I pulled my lists out and found the handwritten number of the funeral home my parents had given me. My hands shook as I dialed. Part of me hoped the funeral home wouldn't answer and I could push this milestone off for another day.

But they did answer. A kind older gentleman answered my questions with compassion that resonated over the cordless house phone. I wished I had a cord to twirl my fingers around the way my sisters had when they were on the phone with a crush. But instead of a cord, my hand was filled with a pen, making notes, and drawing doodles of initials. Though I still had qualities of a young lady, I could feel myself aging. Just making that phone call was more growing up than I ever planned to do. I explained to him that our baby died but wasn't born yet. Every time the word "died" came out of my mouth, it came out in a whisper. As if saying it out loud made it more real. It was already far too real. Nonetheless, one phone call could be marked off my list.

We made the trip to my hometown the next day to visit the funeral home with our little Boston strapped into his car seat and my mom on standby. I knew exactly which funeral home to use — the way any other 20-something does.

It was the same funeral home my family had used for generations. In my grandmother's diary, I read about the daisies at her grandfather's funeral in this very place and witnessed them at my grandmother's.

***

I was nine years old. I put on my navy-blue dress and white pearls; Jackie Kennedy looked back at me when I looked in the mirror. My shoes even had the tiniest heel on them. I wasn't sure what this day would bring, but I was hoping it would send all the visitors home. I needed something to be normal. I needed to visit my grandparents' house without cousins, aunts, and uncles around. I needed a normal day instead of a big deal. I just wanted one more normal day. I didn't know what it would be like now and I needed to know.

The front of the funeral hall had big soft armchairs; two rows of them. Very fancy. The rest of the room was filled with folding chairs. The outside of the room had fancy chairs too, but they weren't in line with where the show was taking place. I had been to visitations before, but never a funeral and if someone had prepared me, I don't remember it now. *What did I need to do to get one of those big chairs?* I know that my grandmother would've given me one. I wanted to sit by Gramps. The people surrounding him felt like security guards. If I were to try to go to him, I'd be intercepted by someone with strong cologne offering me a hug or a piece of hard candy. Nice things that I'd had more than enough of. No thank you. I didn't even want eye contact at that point.

Before I knew it, people had filled the big chairs. Even the folding chairs were filling up now and I started to panic. Everything felt exposed. Those folding chairs offered no protection, and they weren't going to be an option in a minute. My eyes welled with tears. For being surrounded with people that I mostly knew and was related to — I felt very alone. I didn't want to cry with all these people watching and they, too, wanted me to do anything other than cry.

Just as the room started to spin and I was losing the war with my tears, I felt a familiar arm pick me up. My sister's boyfriend. He sat on a comfortable seat built for three people with both of my sisters. I sat on his lap. I found the one person in that room who wasn't consumed with their own grief and could just let me be. I found the sanctuary I needed to let the tears flow.

That may have been the only genuine interaction with him to this day, but I believe some people are meant to flutter around on the outskirts of our lives and us in theirs, never really entering in.

I don't remember any of the words said that morning. I can't recall a single verse read. Despite my grandmother's love of music, the piano was silent that day. Gramps thought it would be more than he could handle. As the line of mourners weaved their way through the folding chairs in order, each offered condolences to my Gramps as they left the room. I did the calculations in my head. We were last. *Were we supposed to be last? Should I cut in line?* Last never felt like something to strive for in my world. I just sat there with the boy who would grow up to be my brother-in-law eventually — too afraid to move.

I looked at my oldest sister with her curled hair and her boyfriend. I looked at my middle sister with her awkward glasses and grown-up dress. I realized they'd always have more time than me — with everybody. I felt incredibly young and overwhelmed.

I watched my parents get up as their turn in line came. My heart raced. *Were they just going to abandon us here?* Just as panic set in for the 15th time that day, my mom turned and motioned to us to follow them. Never had I been so grateful for my mother's hand. She looked amazing that day. What a funny thing to remember—how someone looked at their mother's funeral. Err, their aunt-who-raised-them's funeral.

My mother stood 5'2 on a good day in heels, but she seemed tall at the funeral in her silky dark blue Easter dress. She brushed her

shoulder length brown hair and side swept bangs over her shoulder, for them to just bounce right back. Her eyes were red. She pushed a Kleenex into her other hand to offer her free hand to me.
We entered a very quiet, tiny room off to the side. It was there that my Gramps dissolved into tears in a way I had never seen and never saw again. He gave the tightest, most authentic hug. He was broken for his wife and knew we were too. I felt heard without saying a single word. It was only my immediate family and my Gramps in that room. Maybe a few others, but the important ones were there.

In that tiny room in the funeral home next to where my grandmother's body lay, we filtered out the people on the fringes of grief. In that tiny room I learned so much. Though I spent my childhood surrounded by people I was related to, there was a core of people that truly made up my roots. Those people fit in that tiny room next to the big one in the funeral home.

To this day, when I bake at the holidays or hear St Louis Blues play through the speakers I think of my grandmother. I still long for more time. I wish she'd have known me as an adult or met my husband. I named one of my daughters after her, just so I could keep saying her name. She's still there. I can feel her. I wish my children could too. But she is my ghost to carry now.

***

I carried my grandmother with me, along with the strength of all the people who were part of the making of me as I entered this funeral home once again. It was where I saw my Gramps cry, where my someday brother-in-law saved me, where everything smelled like one specific aftershave my dad wore. But now we'd skip a generation or two and say goodbye to our child there, before even a chance to breathe the air.

It was weird being there in the daylight, the only ones around. We were greeted and immediately taken upstairs. It still smelled like some haunting cologne of a ghost. I had never been upstairs, nor had I considered what might be up there. We entered the interior of what still looked like the bedroom of an old house that had been converted into a conference room. The room was covered in Victorian-looking wallpaper with a floral border. There were heavy drapes on each window with a second set behind it – total privacy. Taking up most of the room was a large conference table, with sterile round edges — the kind of table you picture a big corporate boss sitting at the end of. Chairs that matched the table were rolled up against the dark brown wood veneer and a little more welcoming because of the cushions that adorned them. Just past the large table, my eyes immediately found a door that was opened to a showroom of caskets. Every color of wood and plastic was an option, shiny or matte, dark or light. All kinds of embroidered silks and linens with options for doves and crosses, teddy bears, and American flags, ruffles, flowers. Anything you could imagine that would summarize an entire life in one single box for— forever.

Out of all those options, there were so many things we wouldn't know. We didn't even know if our baby was a boy or a girl yet. The curled position the baby was in on the ultrasound made it impossible to tell for certain who was in there. We'd have to wait for the birth, something my impatient self couldn't have imagined a week or so before. Now we had to consider what the box that would hold the body of my baby forever would have on it.

Sam and I sat on one side of the conference table, with Boston on Sam's lap. I placed three little dinosaur figurines on the table in front of him, hoping that would be enough to distract him while we talked. Part of me hoped he would be a little bit of a distraction, the best kind.

I pulled out three lists of scratched notes, all seemingly very important. I folded and unfolded the lists I held in my shaking hands. We had one chance to make this perfect for our baby. After this — there would be nothing else to do to mother this baby — so every little detail had to be perfect.

We talked about our baby; about the kind of service we'd like to have. We answered enough questions so, that by the end, I didn't feel as if I didn't know my baby. Not only did Sam and I know our baby, but we were the only ones who did. I felt both relief and tremendous responsibility.

Once the obituary had been written, the man opened the door to the casket room, revealing a smaller section of the room. It was filled with small caskets, just as many options —but all tiny. Soft pinks and bright blues, Superman, or rainbows adorned the caskets that could be held by one or two people.

Convinced the baby was a boy —we nearly chose a blue casket, but the funeral director suggested we choose one of each and let him know later. Determined to continue to check things off my list faster than I was adding them, we opted for a tiny white casket with a marble pattern. It was adorned with flecks of gold through the veining and seemed special. With relief, I checked several things off my list: song choices, casket color, verses for the program, things to focus on. These were the things that I *could* do for this baby, where up until this point I only considered all the ways I failed.

"I've been doing this a very long time." The funeral director said in a low tone that was oddly comforting as he gestured to his surroundings. "You might think I'm used to it, but there are still circumstances that get to me." He continued. "There are two kinds of funerals that make my heart break like it's my first day on the job." He paused and handed me another tissue.

"When young children lose their parents and when parents lose their children." As he finished his sentence, he gestured toward us. *Us*, with my round belly that hadn't moved. *Us*, with a bouncing nearly two-year-old happily playing with his dinosaurs. *Us*, who were afraid people would forget. *Us*, who found tremendous comfort in his words. Us, who, in the most surprising of places, had been offered hope. Not the hope of miracles, but the hope of remembrance. Hope, nonetheless.

Our lungs were filled with deep sighs as we left the funeral home. Sighs of relief that Boston had allowed us to concentrate on what was necessary, and sighs of deep, heavy sadness that this was our reality.

There was one more check that needed to be completed before we left town, and it was to choose a monument for the cemetery. One more conversation that seemed to be the same one over and over. There would be more looks of pity, more not knowing what to say, more knowing there was nothing to say.

The headstone we chose had to be one of a kind. We needed it to be special. We picked out a little angel shaped emerald granite marker for our child. We were able to customize the face and features. The only other stone of that shape was sand granite. It had been put way in the back because the shape was distinctly for a child. Nobody, even those headstone shopping, needed a reminder that death came for children too. I felt my skin crinkle and my hair turn gray with each checkmark off my list.

Nine days after watching the heartbeat stop — we found ourselves in the labor and delivery parking lot under much different circumstances than before. The days leading up to this moment, we had spent telling ourselves we wanted some normalcy for our oldest child — but really for ourselves. I was desperate for an escape from the reality that we were facing.

I promised God I wouldn't ask any questions if He would just set it all right again. I knew He could. Between the moments we tried to make normal and the moments we were shopping for a baby's headstone and funeral clothes, it was a place of mental chaos. I walked around for nine days in an out-of-body experience that felt too short and too long all at the same time. I was moving slowly, but the world wouldn't listen. It moved at the same pace it always does —too fast.

We entered the hospital while the dark still engulfed the sky on the morning of what would become the birthday of our second child. When I told the receptionist we were there to be induced, she looked at me and asked me to repeat myself. She doublechecked and seemed confused, looking into my eyes and then back to my stomach.

"The baby died." I whispered, barely audible.

I didn't want to make the joyful mothers around me sad or scared, even though they were across the room — I felt embarrassed. Her demeanor made me feel like I had done something wrong. *Did I?* I retraced every moment of carrying our baby and wondered if I made a mistake somewhere.

We toured home for sale that had smoke damage – was there something dangerous in the air? I continued my running – was it too much? Did I eat enough? Did I eat too much? There had to be a reason, right?

The hospital room door had a small picture of a leaf with a drop of water on it — a raindrop or a tear drop. This image would become permanently etched into my arm with the words "count it all joy" several years later. It signaled that the room was filled with mourners, silence, and sadness.

Willing the heart to start back up hadn't worked. Despite knowing the outcome, we asked for one final ultrasound, just in case. The ultrasound was silent, and the baby was still curled up. It would only be hours now.

The sun stubbornly rose that day. Dark clouds felt more appropriate —but the sky didn't listen. As the light filled the morning, I asked for the blinds to be pulled. Between tears and visitors, the hours crept on, and I went from ready to do anything to keep the baby's body with mine to wanting to see the face, count the toes, end the pain. Nobody had the heart to tell me this was just the beginning. I checked my lists over and over. The checks had mostly been completed. The tasks I had given myself to parent this child were coming to an end. *How could that be?*

I tucked my lists back into my Bible and flipped through the pages, unsure of where to find comfort. I knew it had to be in there somewhere, but it was more than I could manage at the time. Two or three words were the most I could focus on before becoming overwhelmed.

In-between contractions, the snuggles with my oldest child helped. Knowing he would see his sibling and not understand what was happening was always in the back of my mind. I wanted him to have memories, but I didn't want him to remember *this*. The pain was intense. My heartbeat echoed into my ears. My tears never ran dry. Silence and static filled a room where nobody knew what to say. The television buzzed with words no one was listening to. I spent 16 hours in that cold, sterile room just waiting. Even the sheets felt stiff. These are things you mostly don't notice when your baby is born alive.

When I gave birth the first time, we had pored over the playlist. Every lyric mattered, every artist and song was to be the soundtrack for this important event. We hadn't prepared for our second child's birth, and I was glad for the silence. Music was too emotional this time around, and I understood then why my Gramps had decided to leave the songs out of my grandmother's funeral.

The silence didn't break when our daughter was born.

A girl.

Her tiny body was set aside while my body struggled to deliver the afterbirth. I reached for her, and the doctor reminded me to focus. Despite her serious tone, I was only focused on my daughter. I could see her long fingers and long toes as she lay uncovered on a cart next to my feet. The dusting of hair on top of her head was icy blonde.

Her eyes were open and unfocused. She looked cold and I was desperate to hold her, to warm her, to love her back to life.

We had been so sure that it was a brother for our son that now our daughter would be buried with a tiny stuffed blue angel and Boston would have the matching one to keep. I had some post-birth complications the doctor was focused on, but I just wanted to see her face. *Her* face. I couldn't believe it. We kept the same name we'd chosen for a living daughter. Named for both of my sisters' middle names: Keely Rae. It suited her face. Though she was tiny, I could pretend she just looked like she was sleeping after sweeping my hands over her open eyes to shut them. The tiniest wisps of ice blonde hair topped her head. Blue eyes. Long, perfect fingers and long perfect toes. She looked like a little ballerina.

Finally, I held her in my arms, swaddled, and took in every intricate detail. The color of her skin, the shape of her eyes, and the way her little mouth gaped open.

As my body settled down, they took her away for footprints, promising they'd bring her right back. They laid her in the same bassinet that she would've been in if all had been well but covered her face before rolling her down the hallway.

My mom and dad then brought the new big brother into the room. They saw the cart, but not the baby.

"She looks perfect." I told them both.

"She." My mother whispered back, choking on her tears. We shared the name with them, though they already knew. We had to take as many tiny moments as possible for her that we could. So, we shared it again, just to say it. It wasn't long before she was back in the room with us. They had bathed and dressed her and taken some pictures of her in the "butterfly room."

It was a room some broken-hearted mother had made happen so babies who died would have a place to get their pictures taken too. I was grateful for that mother, though I don't know her name or her story. I was relieved to not be the only one to want pictures of my dead child — they were the only pictures of her I'd ever have.

We took the only pictures we'd have of her during that short time. Sam, my mom, and I were the only ones outside of the nurses to hold her. And then her big brother asked. I held him tightly as he held his first baby sister the one and only time — the first and the last. He kept pointing to her little feet.

"So tiny, mama" his bubbly little voice echoed in the room. It could only be met with a tighter hug because the tears outweighed the words.

A nurse noticed my feet crossed at the arches. She said that when they were trying to get Keely's footprints, her feet kept going back to that same position —as if they'd been comfortable in that position in the womb. It was a little glimpse of who she was, and that would have to do. I latched onto those little pieces of her. It's all I had.

We kept her swaddled just as she would've been had she been alive. It was helping to keep the heat from escaping. She was dressed in a little pink robe, with a diaper sprinkled with baby powder — to help her smell like a living baby.

Far too soon, the funeral director arrived. He came himself to take her body back to my hometown, an hour away. I didn't think anything of it at the time, but the nurses told me later that was special — the funeral homes usually follow their protocol. *Who knew there was a usual procedure when a baby dies?* I certainly had never considered that. My heart filled with gratitude that she was special. I knew it, but I loved that other people did too.

As I handed her over to him, my arms turned to lead and my body stopped responding to what my brain was supposed to be telling it to do. *How was I supposed to hand my precious child's body over to a mostly-stranger — to a person I never would've known if she was still alive?*

I kept needing "one more look." I couldn't bring myself to hand her over, so my husband slid his arms into mine, and we did it together. We covered her face with the soft pink felt so she was protected from the eyes of onlookers in the hallway. As the funeral home director turned to leave — involuntary screams escaped. *Utter despair. Torment. The sound of a broken heart.*

The next morning, as I was wheeled down the hallway of the labor and delivery unit on the way to the car, my ears filled with the sounds of crying babies and tired mothers. I noticed one mother standing in the doorframe of her room, cradling her full stomach. She would hold her newborn soon, too, but her baby would look back at her. We made eye contact that I immediately broke.

We got out of there as soon as they'd let me go and escaped into the cold blustery April morning. It had turned cold outside while we were in that cold, dark room. Finally, the weather agreed with me. I hadn't prepared for the cold, so I was wearing the same lightweight black sweatsuit from the day before. I hadn't remembered to bring myself a change of clothes. It wasn't on my checklist.

4

Two days later, we were preparing for the funeral and spent the night at my parents' house. My childhood bedroom was virtually unchanged from the years before. I always found great comfort in the familiarity of that home on "Orchard Hill", especially that night.

I lived in the same room my entire life up until marriage. My American Girl dolls were tucked into their beds in my closet, just as they had been when I was a child. We stayed there with our oldest son, who spent his time spoiled with his favorite tv shows, and filled with extra Easter candy, plenty of snuggles, and toys that covered the main level of my parents' house.

They never would have let me get away with those toys everywhere —I was so grateful. I was grateful for the extra eyes on my son while the haze of grief surrounded me. I was grateful for the safety net my parents always provided. I was grateful my husband, son, and I had a place to go where we could sink into being taken care of.

My dad pretended to be a grizzly bear and chased Boston through the house in his footie pajamas covered in polar bears. I sat on the floor in front of my mom's chair, and she brushed my hair while I rubbed her feet. When it came time for Boston to go to sleep, I would drop rubbing her feet to hold him, but mom continued to brush my hair.

Sam and my dad picked up a board game and played with both laughter and intensity. My husband felt at home here too — it was all over his face. His comfort was found in my parents, in my childhood home — in me. His comfort was in the childhood he was giving our children. We could all take a deep breath here.

Eventually, my mom's hair brushing slowed down, and I heard a snore from above me. On any normal night, I would give her a kiss on the top of her head and carry Boston upstairs to bed. That night, the night before my baby's funeral —I stayed. I stared mindlessly at the television, afraid to be alone with my thoughts. I watched the wedding dress shows switch over to infomercials of sweepers and blenders.

Sam finally convinced me to go to bed, so I gave my mom a kiss on her head. She instantly woke up, just like when I came home from college on weekends late into the night. She would sleep light, until she knew everyone was okay. That night, though, she wanted a hug too. Neither of us were okay.

"I love you, babe" she said, as she patted my face. The tears that were a new constant spilled out of me, but no words came aside from "love you too, mom" — barely above a whisper. I don't know if I ever got to sleep that night. I lay in the dark room listening to my toddler snore and my husband's heavy breath.

I don't know how long it took Sam to get to sleep that night or if his thoughts kept him awake too, but we didn't speak for fear of waking up Boston, and words felt too heavy. The pressure in my chest I had developed was a new normal. "New normal" is a term people like to throw around grief, just because you get used to something doesn't make it normal. It just stops being new.

I got out of bed when the sunlight should've been creeping over the cow fields outside, but it wasn't yet. At the bottom of the stairs, I was met with the aroma of my dad's dark roast coffee. I got my affinity for strong coffee and early mornings from him.

I shuffled into the sunroom of my parents' home where the walls were windows and outside was the yard I played in as a little girl. My playset and bunny cages had been replaced with manicured landscaping and green iron chairs. It was chilly still —the sun hadn't quite reached through the fog. It was peaceful and serene, as Orchard Hill tended to be.

In between our house and "down the hill", as we called my grandparents' home, was total tranquility. My grandparents' home was known to the family as "Pleasant Ridge". Their home sat lower on the hill, about a mile away from the top, where my parents built their home. My mom had made the trek to the top of the hill as a little girl to pick apples and play loudly and wildly with her cousins. Then, as an adult, she made our home there, where we could play loudly and wildly, with a comfort unmatched for the rest of our lives.

The first time I made the trip between the houses alone was by accident. I was six years old riding my bike down our gravel driveway with my middle sister, who was eleven. I was ready to make the hook to the right into the field with distinct tire tracks trail that took us to my grandparents' house and the pool.

As we rounded the first turn, still well within sight of our house, my jelly shoe got stuck. The purple plastic had filled with rocks and jammed into the pedal of my rainbow brite bike.

"PLEASE!!!" I screamed to my middle sister as if I'd been shot. I pulled the bike into the grass although there wouldn't be a car on that driveway until my dad was home from work many hours later.

"COME BACK PLEASE" I screeched.

She was initially about three feet away when she yelled "I can't hear you" and kept peddling. By the second screech, I knew she wasn't coming back, and I knew she was going to get in trouble. *She'll pay for this*, I told myself with the tear-stained vengeance of every Saturday morning cartoon villain. I couldn't get the rocks out of the pedal to make it turn so I started to walk it down the driveway and quickly abandoned that plan. Then, when I turned to take it back up to the house, I made it about five feet before both laziness and excitement overtook the rule saying we had to stick together.

Walking my bike back to the house meant my mom would have to walk me down to my grandparents' and I knew she wasn't ready yet. I couldn't wait —too much to do. I started making my way down the hill, it was about a quarter of a mile and only the cows next door could see me, but in my mind —it was an adventure.

It was the same field that I would ride through while my dad drove in his little jeep, pretending to be WWII spies who'd been found out. It was the same field my middle sister's imaginary friend Sarah the farmer lived in. It was the same field I tried to convince my parents would be a perfect horse field since my mom had horses there growing up.

Across the open field was a huge old tree with sprawling branches. When my mom told the story of sitting in those very woods and reading a book to hide from her sister, that's the tree I always pictured. It's low, strong branches would be sturdy enough to give a boost to a girl that I imagined would look a lot like me — but in a dress of the 50s rather than the spandex slider shorts of the 80s.

The field was ripe with possibilities and deep with family roots. As I skidded my jellies along the rocks and grass —I found God there. I could talk to Him, aloud. I could hear His answers in the blue skies and buzzing nature around me. It was there in that field as a little girl that I started to grow up and develop my own, quiet relationship with our Creator. I felt the hand of God in the world around me, away from the Sunday school worksheets and Bible stories. Out there it was just me and Him.

***

God was there the morning of my daughter's funeral too. Though the day would eventually bring clouds, the morning sun was starting

43

to creep in beams through the fog the way hope glimmers through grief occasionally.

"You ready for a cup, Chooch?" Dad asked as I rounded the corner from the stairs, leaving Sam in bed with Boston. Occasionally Dad still called me by my toddler nickname— usually when he wanted to lighten a mood. It came from the little ceramic train planter set that someone gave my mom when I was born. So, I became "Choo-choo" or the shortened version he used this day. Dad put his arm around me for a hug, knowing the day ahead was bigger than any of us. The ghost in me hugged him back — my body too heavy with emotions to let anymore in. We sipped our black dark roast in the sunroom in silence. The sun rose through the woods behind the house as Dad read the paper — both of us knew he wasn't really reading that day.

After all the planning, checklists, and checkmarks on the completed tasks — I was as ready as I could be. The yearning to hold her a little longer was slowly replaced by a need to let her rest. I feared the final boxes were checked off. And then, what would I do?

How could I be a mother to this baby when all my checklists were complete? What excuses could I find to say her name? I didn't let myself consider these questions until the checks were complete. I could still do *this*. At least.

Sam, Boston, and I left ahead of everybody else for a task I felt too young to be doing. I felt unqualified to face this without my parents but knew they would have been there if we had asked. We didn't ask; they would be there later. It was time for us to face this alone.

We straightened Boston's little blue tie over his pink button-down shirt and let him bring a dinosaur figurine even though scores of people would have candy and hugs for him. We paused at the top of the stairs — just before the door.

What do we do? *Are we supposed to just go in? Do we knock? Do we do the Midwesterner tap on the door, crack it open, and say "Yoo-hoo?".*

I knew that neither of us would yoo-hoo. We cracked the door open and the gentleman who had taken such good care of us in the days before greeted us kindly and led us into the very same room that my grandma Marney's funeral had taken place sixteen years prior.

The room was draped in flowers, more than I had expected. They were encompassing the tiny casket we had chosen which was smaller than I remembered. A man in his black suit led us over to the front of the room and opened the casket. He had laundered Keely's little pink robe. Nothing else would've fit her just right and he wanted to make sure she was beautifully laid to rest. I was relieved to see her the way we had seen her last.

Though life was gone, we studied her face once more. We took in every second and memorized every curve, every hair on her head. Boston wanted to hold her again, but he settled for tucking a little blue angel in the casket with her. He kept the matching one at home. We had been so sure she was a boy.

When it came time to close the casket — I couldn't bring myself to do it. I leaned into my husband, who once again lent me his strength. I melted into a ball of tears and Sam closed it with one hand, while his other arm was wrapped around me.

The next few hours blur together in my memories. Lots of people came — lots of people didn't. Some people from both groups surprised us. It hurt they were absent, but I realize now maybe it was their hurt that kept them away. Even years later, we still haven't seen some of those people. I do remember taking a few breaks to care for my body, which had just given birth and didn't realize I didn't have the fruits of that labor in my arms to feed.

Some people said the right things and others the wrong things. Most said what they thought we wanted to hear, and some said what they felt they needed to say. So many felt like strangers in the room.

I didn't even recognize myself — how could I recognize anyone else? Just before my dad gave her eulogy, our usual wild child Boston curled up in my arms and went to sleep. It was exactly what I needed — an unexpected blessing.

I needed to snuggle a breathing child of mine. I needed to soak in the words of my dad for my daughter. I feared every word said about her would be the last one. I feared every moment was a "last. I held my son in the chairs at the front of the room. These same chairs that had filled up so fast at my grandma Marney's funeral. At that time, I wanted to be in them so badly, and now I understood why I should never have wanted to be in those seats.

When the last verse of "His Eye is on the Sparrow" faded out, each funeral attendee slowly paraded past her tiny casket, and we were led into the little room next to the big room. This was the room where Gramps had broken down in a way I hadn't seen before. I could feel it coming for me too. Something about the last check marks on my list felt final.

As I held my sleeping one-year-old in my arms, I watched from the little room. The friends and family that had cared enough to be there for us lined the hallway to the outside and the lone pallbearer made the walk that suddenly seemed so long. I carried our daughter for her whole life. My handsome, strong husband carried her in death, and it was one of the few times I saw him cry. Tears streamed down his cheeks, but he didn't make a sound. Strong and stoic. He remained strong for me always, to support me, to support our son. As we walked out into the hallways we were met with silence — total silence.

Sam, Boston, and I rode in the funeral car with Keely's tiny casket. We didn't need a full hearse. The procession made its way through my small hometown. I saw my athletic director from high school standing on his lawn with his dog. Then I saw him take his hat off and place it over his chest. I was grateful for the small town I was raised in, and I was grateful that one more person might ask about her and hear her name. Maybe he'd go into my dad's office next week and mention it during small talk. *Maybe Dad would keep her name alive.*

Once we arrived at the cemetery, the weather shifted. A heavy mist settled over the cemetery and a chill was in the air. The top of the evergreen tree that stood proudly over my great uncle at the top of the hill wasn't visible due to the fog. This was the tree my great grandfather planted when they couldn't afford a headstone when their 6-year-old son died. His father-in-law paid for the headstone, but he wanted something from him. So here was the tree nearly 100 years later.

I never related more to that story than in that moment. My heels sank into the side of the hill as we treaded halfway down — next to my grandmother's resting place. The smallest and deepest hole was covered with a tarp. My heart sank right along with it.

I remember only a few moments from our time in that mist. We prayed and sang goodbye to her tiny body. People said nice things and things they thought I'd find comfort in. The songs of praise lifted through breaking voices as I forced the words from the hymn "Near to the Heart of God" out of my throat. I was watching it all from somewhere else, playing a role in a movie. Saying goodbye. Again. Goodbyes to her fingers, to her toes. Goodbyes to her big eyes and pointy chin. Goodbyes to what might have been. A million goodbyes.

Yet, I never really let her go.

On the side of the hill in Oak Grove Cemetery, thinking of my great-grandparents many years before doing the very same thing we were doing — I felt the weight of it all. I felt lines form on my face, a heaviness in my heart I wasn't sure would ever go away. Nor was I sure I wanted it to. I felt older than the people around me, even those a generation ahead.

Boston was awake now, having sung alongside everyone else in the mist of the cemetery. I was grateful to hear his little voice over the crowd. As we got back into the "big car" as Boston called it, the weight of that day lifted a little. Everything went as planned. Keely was buried in the clothes she had worn at birth, thanks to the kindness of our funeral director. *Check.* She was buried with the little blue plushie that her brother had to match. *Check.* We sang the hymns of praise I knew I'd always remember. *Check.* We passed out her name in programs and heard her eulogy, while Boston slept in my arms. Check, check, and a check mark we didn't even know we needed.

Relief, too, came with tears. It seemed tears now peppered every emotion — I couldn't escape them. As the funeral director drove us back to our car at the funeral home, he recognized the series of events as the same relief he sees when mourners return from the grave. A weight was lifted. The boxes all checked off. He prepared us for going forward — reminding us the weight would come back, so enjoy the respite.

He said that not to scare us — but to prepare us. He prepared us for when the shock wore off and we had to move forward.

How could forward even be possible?

We had no other choice. I was never more grateful for Boston's dinosaur facts and games of plastic golf than in the weeks after. I was grateful the cooking shows didn't have baby commercials. I was grateful for the spring air turning warmer. Even through the deepest pits of grief, I was grateful.

5

Exactly one week after Keely's funeral — I found myself at a baby shower for my middle sister. Even though my mom and sisters said I didn't have to go, I knew the longer I hid, the more the pressure mounted to check off "the first time since" box. So, I powered through.

I faked my smile. I gave hugs to people I didn't know. I stuffed tears back in my face when a week-old baby was being passed around. *I could not look at that baby.* Like an out-of-body experience, I watched the baby shower from afar. I was relieved when it was time to go home. Years later looking at pictures, I noticed I still had the hospital bracelets on my wrist. Sam and I kept them on until just before the threads holding them together unraveled.

In those early days when I couldn't bring myself to eat or get off the couch sometimes- I found great urgency to record her face. I buried my grief in painting a portrait of Keely – worried I would forget what she looked like as time went on.

It was cathartic to feel the paint on my fingers when a brush wasn't doing what I wanted it to. The silky paint and the rough canvas danced together to create the grooves of light and shadow. I sketched her face in pencils and charcoal. I mixed oils to find just the right shade of pink that her cheeks might have been if they hadn't gone blue so fast. Her face was all I painted in those early days of grief. I had no energy for anything else for weeks. Grief numbed me to many things, but not this. This was my therapy.

I wanted to be able to share her perfect face someday. Not quite yet, but someday. It would take sixteen years for me to share it with anybody outside those invited into a quiet corner of our home. I traced her face with oil paints the way I had my own finger not long before. Not long, but a lifetime ago.

During this time, Sam and I grew closer to one another and closer to God. I always felt like I had a good relationship with God, but this was different. I didn't want to be the kind of Christian that only came around when I needed something, even though that was still kind of true because I needed Him every day.

I needed the peace only He could offer. I spent time with my Bible alone, no study to follow, no one else around. The urgency I felt to paint and preserve Keely's face was secondary to the urgency to get back to her when my time on earth was done. I studied the Bible, prayed, and praised in song. Sam and I found an even deeper love for one another — the kind of love that happens when you are side by side in the absolute depths of heartbreak and love.

While looking for additional support, I found an online forum for bereaved parents — mostly mothers. I read their stories through tears and then read them again. I wanted to really know them. I looked at their pictures, somewhat jealous that I would never have more pictures of Keely other than one grainy cell phone snap and a handful from the charity that came the night she was born. I saw similarities. I saw differences. I saw broken hearts and more broken hearts.

It took me more than a month of reading stories, posts, looking at photos, feeling called, before I was able to type out the words I would never *really* be ready to share. But once I opened up—this community became my tribe. These were the women I could come to and share how hard it still was, though it hadn't been long at all. I drew courage from the veterans of grief, who had learned to navigate through years of heartache. I saw the stories nobody wants to admit are real — mothers who've buried more than one child. In these stories I didn't find hope — only commiseration.

I don't think anybody is foolhardy enough to actually come out and say, 'It won't happen to me,' but we all, in our glorious ignorance, believe this—until it does happen. Not for fault or fears, not for errors or missteps, but just…because.   Until the unthinkable happens. Again. Mothers and fathers buy a second urn or headstone. They hear a second diagnosis or phone call. They take in so many "I'm sorry"s. After burying your child you don't think, "It can't happen to me", but most of us spend a decent amount of time certain that it will. Again.

There in black and white, on the bereaved parents board, we all lead each other on the road of just making it through. Through grief itself. Through subsequent pregnancies. Through every day, every hour, every minute. The isolation of no one in person understanding my perspective was frustrating but I was fulfilled by those mothers who had been there, were still there, and were going to stay there. We were each other's crutches and confidantes.

I looked at those women as warriors that were put in my path by God Himself to show me that I would make it. There was a light in the tunnel. There may not be an end, but there was light. I looked forward to a day that I could be *that warrior*. When I could be that woman who made other women believe they could survive. I wanted to be the woman who God chose for someone else's path as a helper. There's the light again; that glimmer of rays through the fog.

My mother came to see me at least once a week for the first couple of months to help me with Boston and to help keep up the house. She listened to me on repeat. She walked the boulevard with me when I wanted to walk (though I know she didn't want to). She listened when I needed to talk. She reassured me when I was looking for reassurance.

This woman, who had guided me all my life, spent much of hers riddled in anxiety. But when one of her daughters needed her, she was a pillar of strength. She absorbed my anger when I needed to let it out. I wasn't mad at her. I wasn't mad at God. I wasn't mad at anybody. I was just mad sometimes. She let me be. Then she took my hand and helped me out of it.

She cried with me. She grieved with me. I needed to know that other people were grieving too. I needed to know that Keely would be remembered and not just because I was reminding them. What a terrifying thought to have your child's life forgotten. It was my greatest fear.

At some point, in a tearful conversation that was probably a repeat of others, my mom said to me "I lost my child too."

Me. It was me she lost. The day Keely died, a huge part of me and who I was vanished forever — just like that. And the daughter my parents raised was gone. I was a new person and everybody who loved me had to figure me out all over again. I didn't even know myself anymore, and I didn't care to get to know me.

Before that moment, I had only thought about what I lost. Honestly, I was so deep in grief that I had never considered anything outside my own black hole. But that conversation was a turning point for me. From that day on, I grieved for what my parents lost too, but found determination to find their daughter again.

We needed some normalcy, so I tried to go back to work. Boston needed some time with his Nana, and I needed a distraction. Boston, our dog Mimi, and I would make the hour-long drive twice a week to my dad's insurance agency, where Mom and Boston would play in the office next to mine.

The first day, we made it as far as the Starbucks a few miles from our house before I lost myself in tears again.

"Hey, we've been wondering about you! Did you find out if it's a boy or a girl?" The barista excitedly asked. She knew me by my venti soy latte order and, when it switched to decaf, she knew it was because I was pregnant. I knew her by her sweet disposition and early morning shift. It was the first time I had been back. So, with no one behind me, I put the car in park and spilled my heart to the woman behind the window. She prayed with me. She cried with me. She told me how very sorry she was.

I managed to drive to my hometown, as part of the plan, but I didn't make it to work that day. I'd try another day.

In the weeks and months following Keely's death, I found a new relationship with my mother's mother. My mom was raised by her aunt, who I considered my grandmother. I just called her Marney, but she was my grandmother. I was very protective of that title for her, so considering anyone else my grandmother felt disrespectful to her memory.

Even though I knew my grandmother Marney wouldn't feel that way – I did. It was Marney's sister who had given birth to my mother. But it was Marney who raised my mother and kept watch for my little balloon light in my room as a little girl. She came to grandparents' day at school and was a major part of every holiday. Marney's sister had given birth to my mother, but she answered to "Nana" as a way for me to dodge the grandmother title.

My mother was known to my children as "Nana". Her "grandma" name was a nod to the woman who gave birth to her – a little bit of a redo for them both. She offered forgiveness even when there had never been an apology – reflecting who *my* mother was. The original became "Great Nana", or "Ger Nana" as Boston called her.

Not all the "new normal" that comes out of a death is negative.

***

The year that my Grandma Marney died, my Gramps and I managed effortlessly to weave a new relationship with one another that didn't filter through her. We could grieve alongside one another without ever actually talking about it. It was exactly what both of us needed. We cared for stray kittens in the barn together during that summer. When one would die, we'd name another the same thing and not really acknowledge that there was one less. We'd had about enough of that, thank you very much.

Snowball, Snowball 1, Snowball 2, and Snowball 3 were all completely black cats. Did I mention we also shared the same sense of humor?

I tried to journal because my Gramps bought me a Precious Moments notebook that smelled like cotton candy. He got it for me when he, my mom, and I went on a "field trip" to a monastery. That place didn't have any of the cool weird stuff my 10-year-old mind told me would be in a monastery, but it did have a gift shop.

I started writing poems that were mostly parts of plagiarized Whitney Houston songs, but I think it probably helped some. I continued my artwork in mediums of chalk, crayon, pencil, and whatever pens still worked at my grandmother's desk. Nobody bothered to take down the snowman trimmed in snowflakes with a frosted window artwork that I'd handed to my grandmother early that year. It was titled the eloquent "White Christmas 1990" though we only had a dusting of snow. It wasn't just my artwork that stayed the same — the calendars never updated either.

The sun kept shining that summer. As fall started to approach, my mom found out she got a job as a teacher's aid at my school. She was thrilled. She hadn't worked outside the home since becoming a mom to my oldest sister, who was now a noticeably sassy teen, and we were all getting older.

My mom was a natural at it, and all the teachers loved her. A perk was she shared the same vacation days with us, and she was with me at my school. I rode to school with her every day, and we always got there a "few" minutes late. Mom usually rolled up right as the bell rang.

It was a stark difference from my dad, who felt late if he weren't 20 minutes early. Mom and I took the "back way" to my elementary school that was now my mom's workplace. Rather than the highway to the front of the drop off line, we took side streets through neighborhoods and alleyways.

Next to the railroad tracks near the school was a tiny white house that had a flat front porch with a swing. There was an old man who often sat in the swing — waving to us. Every morning, we would be the same slightly speeding van and he would be the same friendly wave. Mom and I looked forward to our wave back.

The same teacher who went through the line at my grandmother's funeral was the first teacher my mom was assigned to work with. I went there after the last bell of the day rang and ate Laffy Taffy and drew on the chalkboard while my mom finished up.

Naturally, two weeks into the school year — I got the chicken pox. For the first time in my life, I was sick without my mom by my side. For the first time in my mom's life, she didn't have my grandmother to help. So, it was me and Gramps.

My mother didn't know it for about 20 years, but every day of those two weeks, Gramps and I hit the town. We watched a field slowly turn into a Walmart from the safety of his light blue pickup truck parked across the highway. We ate circus peanuts and red licorice while we watched cranes slowly lift materials this way and that. We drove the blue pickup to a friend from church's house and picked persimmons in the backyard. Gramps taught me to give the persimmons a little squeeze, but not too hard or the juice would squish down your wrist.

We cleaned the dust off the grave of my grandmother's freshly set headstone and planted tiny flowers there — those purple crocuses still sprout every year. We picked a few flowers to put at the grave of my grandmother's parents just up the hill from her resting place at Oak Grove Cemetery.

At the top of the hill was the family tree with three generations resting beneath. Gramps and I sat in the dirt that didn't have grass on it yet and listened to the whistle coming from the tree at the top of the hill. We'd sit quietly and never had to wait long. "Woooooooo", we'd whistle back. He put his hand on my shoulder, and I'd never look up at that moment because I knew he was wiping tears with the handkerchief from his front pocket.

In those moments, for just a split second, I'd start to run to my grandmother to tell her a story or share a bite of pudding — then I'd catch myself. I couldn't anymore. She was gone, and I wasn't used to that yet. I knew Gramps wanted to do the same, but neither of us ever mentioned it. So we went about our days, making beef stew and persimmon pudding. We'd eat the pudding before anybody else knew it existed.

Gramps snacked on pig's feet and buttermilk. He'd offer me a quarter if I'd try them, but I told him I'd rather stay poor. He helped me fill in the names of the 92 Indiana counties on my homework without the help of google (because it didn't exist yet) and I could focus on the coloring with colored pencils that went dull much too quickly.

I was sad to see those two weeks coming to an end. Gramps and I could grieve alongside each other without any words, something we both needed. Totally honest grief. I never noticed how easy and how necessary this was until I started to age and understand it more.

What my mother considered a failure because she couldn't be there for me ended up being a blessing. Some of the most special memories I have of my Gramps were made during that time. God led us to those healing moments with those healing people around us —two broken hearts listening to a tree whistle. I wish I had that persimmon pudding recipe now.

The holiday festivities carried on the year my Grandma Marney died. The Christmas trees still smelled the same, the songs were still joyful. Bing Crosby's voice still "buh budda buh buh"d the way it always had. I thought of her often and missed her when certain things came up, like the gingerbread house that was just never quite the same after that.

But it all continued mostly the same to my newly 10-year-old eyes. It took a good 20 years or so for me to reflect on what that year must have felt like for my mom or my Gramps. I don't know why that took so long- maybe the selfishness of grief or the selfishness of childhood and immaturity…or maybe the selfishness of me.

In addition to the buzzing holiday season, our Sunday dinners after church also remained the same. Occasionally, a visitor or two would pop by to see Gramps. I think, too, they wanted to see if the house was still the welcoming place it had always been. They were there on a treasure hunt for hospitality, and I can't tell you with certainty that it ever did feel quite the same to people who were looking for that certain *thing* we were all missing.

Even on the quietest of Sundays, it would be kind of a crowd: my family, my gramps, and my aunt. One Sunday in December, after dinner had been eaten in the quiet between my birthday and Christmas — Gramps was asleep (probably snoring) in his recliner with a football game still on the tv.

Sometimes I'd wake him up by grabbing his arm or loudly asking "ARE YOU ASLEEP?" once or twice to see if he'd play a game with me. He always did. My dad and oldest sister had returned home up the hilltop so he could watch college basketball (hoo hoo Hoosiers) while she waited for her boyfriend to call. I'm sure she loved to soak up the sister-free phone time with nobody to pick up the extension and eavesdrop.

My other sister alternated between napping, reading Sweet Valley High or Babysitters Club, and telling me to shut up. I puttered around drawing on the chalkboard and lining up my mom's childhood dolls in the playroom while my mom and aunt did the dishes. I might have thrown in some New Kids on the Block choreography in there somewhere too.

On this particular Sunday, they called me into the kitchen with *exciting news*. In the 4.3 seconds it took me to go from the playroom to the kitchen, my mind raced with excitement. The news turned out to be that my Nana was coming to spend Christmas Eve night here at Pleasant Ridge. Not long after my Nana gave birth to my mom, she basically switched roles with her sister. Nana always came sometime near the holidays, but never the day of.

My mother and her sister stared at me for a reaction with great anticipation. It was apparent to my 10-year-old self I was supposed to be much more excited than I was. Truthfully, it didn't affect me much at all. I liked her, but I didn't know her. I certainly didn't think of her as a grandmother, and I assumed she didn't think of my sisters and me as her grandkids.

"Oh!" I wasn't sure what to say after that. It was an enthusiastic "oh", but I was late with a follow up. My cover was blown. "Aren't you excited!?" Mom shared her excitement with me, so I garnered some of that. She truly was excited so that was good enough for me. I could tell she wanted me to be more excited and expected me to share her enthusiasm.

"That'll be cool, Mommy." I gave my mom a hug because that was my go-to. I wasn't all that sure what else to do to convince her I was excited.

It felt like they were calling in for backup since my grandma Marney, who had always mustered much of the holiday magic, was now gone. Not just for me, but for everyone. So maybe it wasn't that they were bringing her in for me after all. Maybe they were hoping to glean some magic for their adult selves too. I wish I had followed up that "oh" with more vigor.

Later that afternoon, I flipped through the "Christmas House" album that a cousin had made for my grandmother. It was a collection of photographs from Christmases over the past 40 or 50 years that was not put away with the decorations from the year before.

All the red pajamas on the stairs, lined up for a picture before any presents were opened. Each year, familiar faces. Each year, new faces, changing faces, and many years, some faces gone. I flipped through those pages, mostly looking for pictures of myself —of people I knew. My grandmother was on each page. If she wasn't on a page, it's because she was taking the picture.

"That's me as a little girl." She told me, as I observed a child younger than I was with a bobbed haircut and slight curl. In red pajamas embroidered with *Debra*, her hand being held by a woman I didn't recognize.

"And that's my mother." The calculations swirled in my head. It wasn't my grandmother I was looking at. It was my grandmother's sister. That's when I started to put it all together. My grandma Marney didn't give birth to my mother, but she gave her *life*. She gave my mother a home.

It was my grandma Marney that mothered my mother, but it was my grandmother's sister who answered to "Mom" when my mother said it. This was the first time I started to untangle the web of titles in our family.

"Hmm" I said to my mom. I tucked myself under her arm and listened as she reminisced, taking in the gleam in her eye and light in her voice as she remembered her childhood. My mom always focused on the happy for us. She focused on the sparkle of her childhood. She pointed out the smiles and laughter of the women in the pictures, most of whom I didn't know or didn't know as the young women in the images.

She got lost in stories about Christmas when she was eight and had chicken pox, just like me. She got "baby big eyes" which remained her favorite gift ever. Although I was insulted that the Santa head mug I had gotten her with my own money wasn't her favorite, I was intrigued by baby big eyes.

My mom and I continued turning the pages until we got to the empty ones. They were there for my grandmother to fill up. My heart twisted a little as it does when you realize someone you love will always be missing.

That seemed like a good time to "cheers" with a piece of fudge. Chocolate for my mom and peanut butter for me. The little candy squares still sat by the tin foil train as they always had, so I didn't give any thought to who had made them. They tasted mostly the same.

On Christmas morning we woke up well before dawn as we always did. From the floor of my oldest sister's room, we screeched "MOM AND DAAAAAAD" over and over and over until we'd hear Bing Crosby's voice coming from the record player downstairs. We still weren't allowed to open the door no matter how badly we each needed to go to the bathroom. Our stockings were just around the corner.

After what felt like 1000 hours, my mom opened the door and snapped a picture with her pocket camera while, in the highest 6am pitch she could muster, said "Merry Christmas!". My sisters and I took turns running to the bathroom with our hands to the right of our eyes, so we didn't spoil the surprise.

It was as magical and Christmasy as ever. It was the same as always in my eyes. The sun still hadn't risen when it was time to call down the hill to see if they were ready for us. All my life, my grandmother had been awake most of the night before wrapping presents and making treats – always running behind. As a courtesy, we'd call before showing up on their doorstep before any normal human wakes up. Never once did they tell us they weren't ready.

We'd put our bathrobes over our pajamas and house slippers on our feet. The slippers didn't do much to protect from the cold, but they went with the theme, and we all make sacrifices sometimes — right?

We were greeted at the back door. Holly and garlands adorned…. well, everything. My grandparents' house was straight out of a Dickens novel. I wish I had looked around more the year before. This was the first year without my grandmother. Everyone had worked together to make sure it was as close to the same as it could be without her. Garlands and lights everywhere, the right tablecloths on the right tables, the stockings on the stairs, the tree just tall enough and draped in tinsel. It was as close to the same as it could be that year. And every year after, a little more of the sparkle went out. As it turns out, it wasn't the garlands that held the magic after all, but eventually those went away too.

That was the only year that my grandmother's sister, my Nana, came on Christmas. Maybe she had come in search of a connection to her now-gone sister that she didn't find. Maybe she felt her obligations had been completed with that visit. Maybe she just moved on. I don't recall any discussion about it. She eventually stopped coming near the holidays at all.

Each Christmas morning after that, the sun got higher in the sky before we found our way down the hill. Each year, there were less and less visitors stopping in. Each year, there were more and more decorations that didn't get put out. As I got older, I noticed the differences less and less.

6

Now, sixteen years after my grandmother last tended to the impatiens, another death had forced us all into a fresh start. Every Wednesday morning at 9 am, Great Nana and Great Pop would swing by my house. He was heading to his retired men's group to hang out and Great Nana was coming with us. We would load the car up with Boston's stroller and stop by a little local coffee shop for black roast coffee and a walk along the river. I got to know Great Nana as more than my "real" grandmother's sister. I got to know her for more than the mistakes she made as a young woman. I got to hear her stories about the lighter side of that wild youth that had defined her for me until now. I got to hear her talk about the grandfather that I was supposed to look like but would never meet. I got to hear about her life from her perspective. It gave me something to focus on that wasn't death. It gave me something to focus on that wasn't sad or heavy. I got to picture her dancing along the very riverfront we were walking along, but as a teenage girl that wasn't allowed in a Frank Sinatra concert.

One of those Wednesdays, I got an early call from the bereavement counselor at the hospital. She said she had something she'd like to bring to me. I glanced around at my house knowing it wasn't ready for visitors and mentioned that to her. She assured me she not only didn't want me to clean, but she would also be upset if I did.

"You are doing the most important work you have to do right now…grieve." Her voice and demeanor were comforting, but I was still hesitant.

I reluctantly agreed to her stop over and, before I was even off the phone, my Nana was on her feet with a broom in hand.

"No, Nana, you don't have to do that!" I tried to assure myself that the bereavement counselor really wouldn't notice, but I was so grateful for my Nana's presence right then. She and Boston, with his tiny matching broom, swept the floors and picked up toys together. I got myself ready-ish for a visitor.

I had a passing thought of throwing away the dead flowers on the shelf from well-wishers, but I wasn't ready. Surely, she would understand if I didn't. She brought over a memory card with copies of the only photographs we'd have of Keely, and box of mementos —tangible things for mothers who won't have many tangible things for their babies. Most of the trinkets were homemade by other mothers who had suffered similar loss before me — finding a way to pay healing forward. She also brought over an excuse to say Keely's name and a distinct memory of my Nana supporting in a way that she hadn't before, but I desperately needed now.

I started a tradition of making pumpkin muffins for our Wednesday visits and sending them home with my Nana. We'd each eat one and pack the rest away for when Great Pop came to pick her up. They went perfectly with black coffee and the windy riverfront. If it rained, instead of a stroll on the riverfront, we'd drive around until Boston fell asleep in his carseat and then park at the river. We'd drink our coffee and watch the raindrops hit the water. The waves usually rose to meet the rain on those days.

She would distract me from my fears with stories of her wild youth. The stories were entertaining when you could dismiss the hurt her mistakes had caused over the years. I think part of her spent our time together trying to make up for it, and it worked. I got to know her as a new person. God allowed me the opportunity to know her not by her youthful mistakes, but for the person who was formed by them. It wasn't a second chance for me, it was the first chance I had gotten to know her for who she was. God placed us there together on those Wednesdays with a great purpose.

A couple of months into grieving Keely, we all settled into a new routine. Boston, Mimi the dog, and I were making our twice a week trek to my dad's office. We'd stop for a Starbucks on the way and the same barista would excitedly acknowledge when I ordered a decaf coffee.

"Ohhh, does this mean what I think it means??" referring to hopes I was pregnant again.

I met her excitement with anticipation of my own and shared with her that we'd know in a couple of weeks. I was being overly cautious, as if there were such a thing.

A few weeks later, when I ordered regular black coffee and hoped she wouldn't acknowledge it, she didn't, aside from a sympathetic smile and silly comment about the Baby Einstein videos. I was grateful.

I looked forward to the weeks that I would be able to join her in her hopeful excitement. This virtual stranger to me, who knew nothing more than my regular coffee order, looked forward to my good news. I looked forward to sharing it *someday*. I prayed for the day that my decaf order would continue. I prayed for the day I saw a second line on a pregnancy test, and I could scream it from the mountaintops one more time. I was grateful for the support of this acquaintance because she knew what we had been through, and I didn't have to explain any more. She wasn't forced into the trenches with us because she loved us – she could just cheer us on from the sidelines.

It wasn't my time yet. Every week, every cycle seemed endless. In the meantime, my sister gave birth to her first child. A daughter. We did not have a chance to daydream about how much fun those two girls would have together. Now we never would.

Those months waiting to conceive again felt like an eternity. I had aged immensely — both in heart and head. We searched for answers with a team of doctors and, when faced with the possibility of finding them, felt unsure about *wanting* to know. I started the search desperate to know and soon realized that it wouldn't change her being here, but it may end up changing our possibilities for the future. I didn't trust unknowns. I didn't trust the known either. I didn't trust much, but I did trust God.

Everything doesn't happen for a reason. My child didn't die for a purpose or a punishment, but He could use that grief for great gain. That was the best I could do then, to go forward, to do well, to have the hope of seeing our girl again someday. My bargaining with God hadn't worked out, but it didn't stop me from trying again. Through the deep grief, I forged a new relationship with God.

He was the same God I got to know on the walks between my parents' and grandparents' houses. He was the same God whose presence I felt when I rose from the waters in the little country church a changed girl. He was the same God that offered His comfort in my darkest hours. All good and perfect gifts are from above. All imperfect people have great purpose in His hands.

He was unchanged. I was new. I was new and unsure who I was for now. I only knew that I had changed. I feared I would join the ranks on the bereavement board of mothers who suffered loss once, and then again. It was a simmering fear buried beneath a deep desire to have another baby. I wanted to see Boston as a big brother to a living child. I wanted my children to be close in age. I wanted my family to grow in a way strangers could see too. I wanted my arms filled with the sounds and smells of a baby again.

I searched for answers with the medical team with a hand over my face, peeking through. *What if the answer meant it would happen again? What if more babies weren't in our future? What if we could have saved her if we had known?* I searched for answers from God. I came to understand that there were none. That would have to be okay. That would have to be the answer. I wasn't sure I wanted to know, but that didn't stop me from googling.

Summer passed painfully slowly that year. The summer sun was sprinkled through the full leaves in the trees. The sounds were pools splashing and sprinklers chattering. What would have been Keely's first summer was filled day by day with a calendar check of survival.

Each day marked by whether I was pregnant again and how quickly I could be. Wednesdays were marked by the riverfront walks. Evenings were marked by how quickly Sam could get home from work so we could all walk down the boulevard from our house. It was during those evenings Sam and I allowed bits and pieces of hope to sneak into our hearts.

In June of that summer, Sam, Boston, and I found ourselves at Best Buy and I found myself ogling the cameras. Window shopping had become a free time tradition.

"Get it." My husband said with forceful encouragement. We both looked back at the $1200 starter camera body and kit lens.

"Get it." He repeated.

My heart fluttered. It was fun to think about something else. I was not thinking about if I was pregnant or not — this moment of respite was such a relief.

"I don't want to put pressure on our money." I responded, hoping he already had an answer in mind. I was usually such a planner, full of lists and preparedness. We had not planned for this. I had not researched this.

"Don't worry about that. You'll make it back." He already saw the hesitation on my face and followed it up with "Even if you only ever make half of it back, we'll have pictures of Boston."

"And our other kids" he continued. "Family pictures."

"But you'll make it back." He was so sure. He was far surer of me than I was of myself. I didn't want the pressure of that price tag. He knew my buzzwords. *Family.*

Sam soon picked up the box and handed it to me.

"Get it."

I didn't want the pressure of the price tag, but the thought of something to pore myself into was so tempting. The allure of something I could focus on lead me to the front of the store. Photography pun completely intended. Little did we realize then the impact that $1200 purchase would have on our future and on our family.

If I had known then what I know now, I would have strutted to the front of the store like a peacock, proud of all the things to come. That day, though, we were taking a risk. In that box was the seed of my business.

In that box was art therapy that would help me work through all the best and worst moments in my life. The price tag was the exact amount of pressure I needed to make myself come through for my family. God knew I needed the pressure. My husband knew it too.

As July came around, I began to focus on Boston's second birthday party. I prayed I could give him the gift of a living sibling on the way, but the months were running short. Great Nana and I talked about it on our walks. My mom and I talked about it on the phone and when she came to visit. It was a fun distraction. It was a frustrating distraction. Time moves so slowly when you were ready a year before.

Then we got a phone call from my dad.

My father's father, my grandpa, had been suffering. He had gone from moments we thought he was teasing us, like not recognizing me at my high school graduation to not acting like himself at all. Then, he went on to him not recognizing anyone. He spent his final years starting a new life every morning under the care of the memory loss team in a nursing home. Sometimes he recognized the love of his life- sometimes he didn't. She spent some of his final hours at the county fair- I think afraid to face the reality of it all. It had been a long goodbye.

The call that he passed on wasn't a surprise to anyone, but the finality always does seem to shock. "Prepared" becomes so sudden so very quickly.

Sam had used all his time off to say goodbye to our daughter and grieve. He had been allowed 3 days to bury his daughter. They weren't about to give him time to honor his wife's grandfather.

Boston and I made the 3-hour drive two days in a row to be home with Sam at night. I didn't mind the drive. I was more okay being alone with my thoughts than I had been in a while. We could play music or listen to the Baby Einstein DVD that was the current favorite. On the way out of town, I updated our favorite Starbucks barista on our private life events. I still didn't know her name. I knew her face and felt like I knew her heart.

Everything was heavy again. It was different this time, as weight tends to be when it's all spread out with a long goodbye. I loved my dad's father and would miss him, though I can't say I knew him that well. At the funeral, Boston fell asleep in my arms again. He made it easy for me at yet another funeral. I was so grateful. He let me listen to the preacher talk of Grandpa's responsibility to God.

The man spoke of my grandfather losing responsibility as he lost his coherence. Boston's sleep let me listen to the muffled sounds of the funeral in the next room singing "I'll Fly Away" much better than if we all were singing it. I sat in a room of people that had been sad for my grandfather for a long time. Little moments of forgetfulness adding up to a time he was a new man that nobody knew, himself included. The goodbyes and the tears started years beforehand. Now was a sense of relief that he was whole again. We could rest in my grandfather knowing God. We could rest in hope for him. We could rest in his rest.

It was a much different scene than we'd witnessed just four months prior. This death was sad, but this death was in order. Had it come four months sooner- I don't know what my reaction would have been. Everything was viewed through a haze of sadness already. This death was as expected as a final goodbye can be; maybe with even a layer of relief that his suffering and confusion was also laid to rest. I was mostly sad for my own dad. Sometimes it's always too soon.

My soon-to-be two-year-old son had become too accustomed to death and funerals. I prayed for a break for him. Some of those funerals celebrated accomplishments of a life well lived. Others mourned accomplishments that never got to happen — the untapped potential of all the little and big moments. Some were filled with gratitude, some with regret —many are a mix of both.
We focused on Boston's second birthday to celebrate what we did have, and to take the attention off trying to conceive, at least we tried to. Lurking in the back of my mind was always how close we could be to having another baby. I felt frantic. I prayed. I bargained with God. I know that isn't how it all works — I tried anyway.

For each pregnancy test I took, I held it up to the light and examined it closely. Each morning brought disappointment. Each afternoon brought hope for the next. Boston was a big brother and the ache to give him a playmate was constant.

Our Starbucks visits continued as normal. Each decaf order brought us closer to the possibility of good news. Every day felt a year closer to the day finally coming. Time moved slowly.

My mother and sisters were coming to town to visit for the day. We planned to go to the mall, and maybe have lunch there. We planned to meet with Nana and let the kids play in my backyard. I *daydreamed* the days before about being able to tell them in person I was pregnant. Our mall shopping would shift to a onesie or teddy bear. I daydreamed that I'd be able to keep a secret in the hour it took my mom to drive to my house. I daydreamed.

I fantasized about it so much that when the morning rolled around, I *expected* to see two lines appear on the pregnancy test. What a dangerous scenario for a broken heart.

My hopes began to sink. One line. I'd just wait longer. Still one line. Tilt it to the light, squint my eyes, take the back off the test, hold it up for some secret code line. Still one line. Although it wasn't the first pregnancy test to let me down that week, it was the first one to make me cry. I folded myself up in the hallway of our little home with my dog and cried deeply. Boston, just barely two-years old, ran by blissfully unaware and unfazed.

All the scenarios I had gone through in my daydreams were ghosts to our real day —like a parallel world to what I had envisioned. It was a never-ending cycle. By the end of the day, I was calculating when we might be able to try again next month. *When would the baby be due? When would we feel "safe"?* I hadn't let myself realize yet the time we could relax was never going to come.

Once we arrived at the mall, my eyes immediately went to every pregnant woman —every baby onesie. I know it was written on my face, even though I couldn't get the words out. But my mom knew, she always knew. I snuggled my baby niece, breathing in her newborn scent and feeling the weight of her tiny self in my arms, with a bittersweet pang of who they might have been together- a dynamic cousin duo the way Boston was with my nephew.

The next morning, I skipped my usual pregnancy test routine. It was plenty late enough in my cycle and I just couldn't stand it again. I had been so sure this time — so much for motherly instincts — mine were broken. Three days later, God found a way to sneak hope back into my heart. I told myself I might as well use the pregnancy tests I was hoarding.

One line. I let more time pass to allow my heart to settle into disappointment again. Another look, still one line. I tipped it towards the light. One line. I took it into the kitchen light and tilted it again.

…. wait a second.

The slightest shadow of a second line. I screeched. If I could've thrown a parade at that moment I would have. I screamed for my husband and showed it to him. He met my excitement with confusion. He wanted me to be right, but he didn't want to break my heart with honesty.

"What are you looking at?" he asked cautiously. "There are supposed to be two lines, right?"

"WHAT?! YES!!" *Why was I still screeching?* Pure elation.

"What are you looking at, babe?" Sam questioned. I demonstrated how to hold the test in just the right light and tilt it with precision to reveal that sweet, sweet second line.

"Okay, I see what you are talking about, but that doesn't count." He watched my face and was careful with his words.

My hands shook as I took a picture and posted it on my moms' group online. They'd see it. They knew how to tilt it to the light just perfectly. So many of them had been where I was right at that moment. I needed someone else to see it too. I knew what it was. I could see it. I could *feel* it the week before. I had been too impatient, but now there it was as clear as it could to be to me.

As I waited for responses on my post, I called my mom and felt like I had to tell her with the caveat that Sam didn't see it.

"Oh gosh, babe. When will you know for sure?" she questioned. She also was afraid to get too excited.

The responses on the moms' board started to roll in.

"I hope it's there, but I don't see it."

"Sorry mama."

"Have you tilted it to the light?"

"Take a better picture; this one is blurry."

"Maybe it's the picture, not the test."

I still saw it. As the time passed, the test became clearer to me. I needed another test, so I chugged just enough water that I could test again without diluting it. It was starting to sink in again— hope. We could have hope with a due date again. I just needed everybody else to see it too. When I went to take another test, there were none. Turns out I went through them all. I used them all up on negatives. What a waste.

I ran to the drugstore while Sam stayed home with Boston. He left me unattended, and I came home with six pregnancy tests from two different brands. I had become a connoisseur of pregnancy tests. I knew which ones were the most sensitive. Blue dyes, pink dyes, time limits, cycle days — I knew which ones were the most reliable. I had amassed hours of internet research. I had some I felt were lucky. I ignored the negatives that those brands had given me.

When I arrived back home, Sam was cooking lunch. We gave each other a kiss and I went to the desperate work of proving there were two lines on that test. I was not coming out of that bathroom until I had some cold hard facts to show the world.

The early test, the expensive one, was my best bet. That first line appeared immediately. I knew I had to wait for the second one; I was trying to jump the line on what constituted an early pregnancy test.

Just about when time stopped moving— I saw it.

Two beautiful, visible lines. I screeched.

I ran into the kitchen where Boston was in his highchair and Sam was at the stove. I strutted into that kitchen and told Boston outright.

"You are going to be a big brother AGAIN!" He raised his hands over his head, his face covered in the crumbs of lunch and cheered with me. Finally, someone to cheer with me again. Sam turned to me, still skeptical. I held up the new Rolls Royce of pregnancy tests in front of the endless smile spreading over my face.

He very calmly turned to put his spatula down and turned back to me to give me the biggest, tightest hug. Without fear, there would be no courage. For the first time in a while, I let the courage be louder.

I spent the next two weeks telling everyone in the world with the unfiltered joy of someone who didn't understand that there were no guarantees in life – pregnancies, babies, life. I was determined that I would celebrate this baby, this life, for as long as I had it with me. Even through paralyzing fear, the hope was more vibrant, more powerful than I would let fear be — at least for now.

The elation in my voice reverberated through the drive thru as I ordered my usual coffee, but *decaf* with emphasis. I was hopeful that our regular barista would be on the other end. By the time I pulled around to the window, both of us were crying. She pumped her arms in the air and didn't charge for my decaf.

"Confirmed??" she asked with sheer excitement for this stranger that had been taking her on a daily roller coaster for months.

"YESSSS" I squeaked out as my voice got higher and more tears of happiness and relief fell. I could celebrate easily with this person who knew so much of our story but wasn't personally invested in it. I couldn't let her down.

The triumph of that second line was followed in the coming weeks with a range of other emotions. Hope, caution, fear, pessimism, optimism, more hope, more fear. *This is happening.*

Many of those emotions were sprinkled around one another, like playdoh after you mix colors. In my life after Keely, I was different and so were the emotions that felt so black and white before. *Could I let myself feel hopeful? Would this baby live? Would I ever take a deep breath again?* The intuition that I was so proud of was failing me now. I was sure this baby would die too.

7

Each doctor's appointment brought tremendous relief with the sound of a beating heart. Each hour that passed after would allow just a little more dread to creep in until the next doctor's appointment heightened the roller coaster again. Luckily for me (I guess?), there were plenty of doctor's appointments this time around.

I had the specialists, ultrasounds, at home doppler, and biweekly appointments for the entirety of the pregnancy — sometimes more often than that. None of those things brought me peace, though. At least not lasting peace. The fleeting peace of relief would have to do until we could have this baby screaming in our arms. Every day, I prayed this would all end up right. Every night, I prayed.

In the in-between moments, I prayed. I promised to be better if God would allow this child to live. The only sleep I could find would be at the end of a prayer. Sometimes I would let God know early in the prayer that I needed Him to allow me to sleep. I leaned into the Psalm that reminded me to lie down and sleep in peace. I leaned into the knowledge that God already knew.

I, along with the community of online bereaved moms I relied on, repeated to myself "most babies live" day after day, sometimes minute after minute. We reminded each other when it was easy to forget.

We celebrated cautiously throughout the holidays that year. Everything had a caveat now, an asterisk. I tried to not get too attached to the child growing in my womb. I wanted to wait until it was safe to love again. I failed at that. I couldn't help myself. Every minute of every day was spent in hopeful prayer that my body could sustain the life it was creating; the life I already loved with every fiber of my body.

We found out that our rainbow baby was a boy. He would carry the name we had chosen for Keely if she had been a boy. It meant "dove" and that seemed so peaceful. Callum Robert, middle name after his daddy. Sam, the boy I had thought was so arrogant the day I met him, didn't want a child named after him. I desperately did. We landed on a compromise —his middle name, which was his grandfather's name.

Each ultrasound that mirrored his big sister's scared me. I loved how much he looked like her, but it scared me that it was a sign. Everything scared me. Each day left me surprised by my own reactions to the world, to the day's events, to life. The clock ticked louder and louder.

Each day was met with "this day last year" memories that were bittersweet. Our time with Keely alive was now marked by her death. Our time with Callum was now marked by how old his sister should be. We were clouded by fear and grief, and what should have been and what shouldn't have been.

Alongside our grief was elation. Alongside our grief came a deep, profound love for what we did have right here, right now in our arms. We carried a gratitude that we had the time we did with Keely. I would rather have a broken heart than one not filled with knowing her. We fully came to appreciate the intricate miracle that every life is. Grief was often louder and seen more by others, but the love was so very abundant. We were so ready to hold another live baby in our arms.

We knew our rainbow Callum would come early. The specialists we were working with didn't want to take any chances. Sam and I couldn't agree more. Despite the scheduled early arrival, I wanted that baby to come out as soon as it was safe for him. As soon as his lungs were ready, so were we. Every stomach pang brought a timer to my attention. As the anniversary of Keely's death approached, I wanted our baby boy to come on out. None of the old wive's tales worked. The spicy Japanese noodles that I was so sure were the jumpstart to Boston's labor were eaten with anticipation with no such luck.

We stood at the cemetery honoring her one year to the day after she died. It was cloudy with a chilly breeze but otherwise a peaceful day. Every memory I have from then was cloudy. I don't know if it was actually darker weather that year, or my own recollection added the clouds. We sent pink balloons into the sky along with a character balloon Boston was sure she'd love. Tacky as it was, he just may have been right. We'd never get to know for sure. Wind gusts picked up the balloons and sailed them past the tree my great grandfather had planted. One of the balloons stuck high in the branches of that family tree, then another. The wind continued to whip them until they both had loosened back into the sky. I felt compelled to stand and watch to make sure they both got where they were supposed to be – back into the sky. Time slowed down under that tree for a while.

Our rainbow baby boy's birthday was chosen by our doctor, on a day that worked with her schedule. My mom and dad arrived before the sun was up. They were going to stay behind with Boston for a few hours so he wouldn't be so tired during the biggest moments that we expected to be much later in the day. We didn't know how long to expect. As we pulled out of the driveway, waving goodbye to Boston and my parents, I was overwhelmed with emotion. Tears poured down my face. I was sad to be away from our little big kid, but every emotion that I could think of overtook me.

The entire last year was so…much. Now we were faced with what could be the hope we'd been searching for- a screaming, breathing baby that could look back at us. I looked forward to a moment I could fully enjoy again. I looked forward to the peace and elation that comes with the first sounds after a living birth. I looked forward to seeing our children meet each other for the first and not last time. I looked forward.

But still — I wanted to bring her with us. I was terrified that she'd be forgotten. I knew I wouldn't. I knew Sam wouldn't. But I needed everybody to remember, to talk about her, to relate her to her brothers. I didn't want her left behind because it would make us sad. I feared the best-intentioned avoidance.

As we got closer to the hospital, anticipation settled into pure excitement. I had a burst of energy that shamelessly propelled us past the other two couples that were clearly heading towards the labor and delivery department. Like a 6 AM mall walker, my gigantic belly and I charged past everyone else as they paused to breathe through a contraction or two. I guess it was a benefit of being induced.

We went through the same doors we had left empty armed through just a year earlier. It felt like both yesterday and an entire lifetime all at once. We went to the desk to sign in and were soon led down the same hallway. For something so familiar, it was so very different this time. The nurse that was just ahead of us read the room number seemingly to herself.

"Oh God" I prayed under my breath that I'd heard wrong.

Sam grabbed my hand. Just as we got to the door that was the very same door, the very same room that had our sign with a teardrop and leaf on it the year before, he said in a low tone to our nurse "Our daughter was born still in this room last year."

Immediately, her face softened, and she moved us to the room nearest the nurse's station. Her name tag read Michelle. I would be very grateful to Michelle more than a few times over the next 48 hours.

My doctor —the same that had delivered Boston and Keely- came in to check on us before heading into surgery. She wasn't very talkative, but I made up for it, filling the air with nervous chatter. I was anxious and excited and anxious and excited and repetitive.

I placed my Bible on the tray across what was left of my lap, just as it had been during Keely's birth. This time, however, rather than the 23rd Psalm, it was open to Jeremiah 29:11. God already knew.

Sam turned on the playlist of soulful folk music we'd put together to help bring us peace and anticipation rather than letting fears creep in. We hoped the songs would both keep us focused and distract us. We spent those early hours trying to watch house hunting television shows and listening to music, but time moved so very slowly.

As hours passed and labor progressed, my parents and Boston came. The contractions were getting stronger, but I knew we had some time. I opened my eyes after breathing through one to see a little foot dangling next to me with a Spiderman croc hanging off it.

"Mom, you didn't" I had to laugh…

In my best efforts to keep my child dressing to the nines as a newer mom — I drew a hard line and forbid crocs, even though my mom was famous for her croc'd feet. At one point, she took her sweet time telling her grandbabies goodbye in the parking lot of a school play as a thunderstorm rolled in. We teased her mercilessly that lightning would reduce her to smoking crocs if she waited too long.

She was also famous for her feet being sore, so all the teasing was in good fun since she found some shoes that helped keep her feet happy. She must have planned to wait until I was in active labor to take Boston to Target and let him "talk her into" Spiderman crocs. You know, because regular crocs would be too subtle. To this day, a single Spiderman croc is tucked into the baby book of Boston's to commemorate my mother's devious croc-loving spirit.

It was just the fun, lighthearted laughter I needed as the pains got more intense. Boston continued his gleeful toddlerhood through more adult anxiety than most adults face. Here he was, bringing the sunshine once again. As my labor intensified, the more worried I became. The excited anticipation turned to just old-fashioned anxiety. I needed to see his face, hear his cry —see his chest raise and lower.

My sister, who was recording Callum's birth, forgot to stop it when she put the lens cap on. That's how I remember it as well, though with glimmers of picture. There were unintelligible words, gasps, oohs, ahhs, tears, muffled sounds, and sheer emotion of every variety. The moment I saw his chubby face, just as his brother and sister before him, he filled a spot in my heart that was made for him. Hearing his cry and to see his eyes looking back at me filled me. My heart was both broken and filled a thousand times over.

Every beautiful moment we were blessed with was one Keely was missing from. We knew she was there; I could picture her. I wanted other people to see her too. Ecclesiastes 3 kept rolling through my mind: "For everything there is a season, a time for everything under Heaven. A time to be born and a time to die." My heart remained grateful for the time we had, both past and present and, Lord willing – the future too.

The next day, rolling down that hallway as we left the hospital, I felt so triumphant. It hadn't been that long since the tear-filled journey that took me down that same route before, but it had been a lifetime all the same. Sam already had filled the car with balloons and flowers of congratulations. I held our new baby in my arms and our toddler skipped alongside the wheelchair my husband pushed me in. From the outside looking in, it was picture perfect.

As we rolled down the hallway, I looked for the mothers without babies in their arms. I looked for someone who was now where I had been the year before. I knew the statistics well enough to know there was probably a broken heart close by. I didn't see any though — not that day. I don't know what I would have done had I seen a newly bereaved mother. I don't know what I would've said or done because even when you've been that mother, finding the right words is an impossible task. But I looked for her in solidarity — maybe to offer her hope or an ear to listen, and maybe to prove to myself I wouldn't forget.

We spent the next few weeks figuring out what life looked for a family that had focused solely for the last nine months on adding to it. We soaked in every sweet baby sound he made. We took pictures of every snuggle he got from his big brother. We noticed every butterfly that April held and assumed that was a visit from his sister. We hoped for a peace that we were unwilling to admit would be different now. We had peace, but the kind of peace that settles around a wound after trauma. *Maybe now we could focus on living.*

8

"Everybody's dead." my Nana said in a moment of deep clarity from her hospital bed. It didn't seem directed at me, even though no one else was in the room. "Hmm" she continued, still not to me.

She was watching the slideshow of the 4000 slides that I had digitized on the TV. I had just finished scanning them the week before. My grandmother Marney had photographed and cataloged thousands of images over decades and decades of family gatherings and vacations, and I was in a hurry to get them to her to help her pass the time. I was so sure she'd be going home soon. She teared up as we flipped through the same pictures. As a little girl, I didn't know some of the people in the photos, but I started to learn more about them as an adult.

The little bouquet of azaleas I cut from the flowering shrub at my house sat in a plastic cup of water in her hospital room. She always admired them, and I didn't want her to miss them this year. Just enough of a gesture, not over the top. I didn't want to signal that I thought anything was wrong. She sure didn't seem like anything was wrong.

"Aly." she had snapped back to a conversation with me at this point. "You know all the things that are important to me, right?" I thought she was getting ready to start a list of things that were important to her life, so I waited.

"For my funeral." She continued.

I was stunned. More than a few times, the Wednesday conversations on those walks would turn to death. My Nana recalled her own mother's funeral. As my grandma Marney, my Nana, and their third sister stood next to their own mother's open casket, they heard an elderly woman say "She's really put on some weight" referring to their newly dead mother's body. This was a driving force in her wanting to be cremated.

"I'll be the smallest I've ever been!" she gleefully joked each time she told that story, considering her lifelong battle with her weight. "Nobody needs to see this body anyway. I've given them plenty of chances." She giggled at her own jokes as we continued our walks throughout the last few years. In those years since Keely died, I had given birth to Callum and then 2 years later, another baby brother Beckham. He was born just before Christmas, so we hadn't gotten back into our walks yet, waiting for winter to ease its grip on the air. Now in the hospital, the jokes didn't land.

Of course, we had talked about all her final wishes. This was a someday conversation not a today conversation.

"Yes, but it'll be a long while before any of that is important." I answered, nearly in the form of a question.

"Right?" Okay, now it was officially a question because she was making me nervous.

"Why are you talking like that? Are you nervous?" I asked, with my own nerves tucked into the question.

"Well… someday." She kind of trailed off. I didn't press further. Even as someone comfortable with chatting about death, it felt too close right now.

"Yes, Nana. I know." I hoped to ease her worry, but I don't think I did.

I was on borrowed time to get back to my nursing baby, so I leaned down to hug her, and I told her I'd see her after she got settled in at home. We both thought she was going home the next day. Walking out of the hospital as the sky started to turn darker and purple, I felt great relief. Not only did I feel like I had done what was expected of me, but what I needed to do. I looked forward to bringing her pumpkin muffins, even in April, towards the end of the week.

Going home didn't come the next day like we anticipated, or the day after that. The blood cancer they told her the year before wouldn't kill her was doing just that. With each visit, she was declining. Though I saw her most days throughout that month, I regretted not bringing baby Beckham to see her one more time – he was 4 months old now. Maybe sweet baby magic was just what she needed.

During one visit, she was frantic. She was terrified of dying. She wanted me to bless her the way a Catholic priest would. I am neither Catholic nor a priest. I prayed with her. I prayed for her. I hoped for her. I saved my tears for home. She needed comfort. Though she was sure she was dying, we weren't so sure. The doctors had a plan. Why would they plan anything if she was dying? I told myself with ignorant hope. New information along with a new plan, came daily and through a game of telephone with family members. Looking back now, I think she chose to withhold the truth from us to make the goodbyes more bearable.

A year and a half after the birth of our rainbow baby Callum, Sam and I found ourselves expecting a new baby. He was born just before Christmas. I reveled in having a December baby, just like me. Those were the bright moments. Those were the moments I could just be an excited young mother — expecting a new little bundle. In darker moments, and always in the back of my mind, was the knowledge that *expecting* it all to go a certain way wasn't realistic.

In some moments, I was paralyzed by fear — others by hope. I spent the extra doctor's appointments grateful and appreciated the extra eyes on our new baby.

During each appointment, my own heart stopped until I saw the baby's heartbeat strong. I was both nervous and excited to see my boys become big brothers, and Boston for the third time. I lamented that I couldn't see Keely's reaction — even though my heart said I could.

It was during my pregnancy with Beckham that my Wednesday walks with Nana stopped. Boston's July birthday party was at the zoo, where Nana splashed through the sprinklers with her great grandsons. She joked that she could "die happy now" because the day had been so special to her. She continued that she might die if we had to walk up one more hill. This day was also the catalyst for my modified bedrest. I was limited to 4 hours of activity per day because my doctor thought just limiting my activity to four hours a day would be enough to allow my body to do its most important work. My days of walking on the riverfront were on hold for now. Even daily and necessary tasks had to be limited.

Thankfully, excluded from my four hours was painting — provided I painted sitting down. I was working on memorial paintings for friends whose children had died, and word spread to others in the bereaved community that started out as strangers to me. How could they stay strangers when I spent many hours staring at their loved ones' faces. I set up my paints next to Boston's little easel. With Callum in his highchair and paints of his own, we spent several hours each week focusing on the contouring of a baby's face or the color of the favorite blanket. We listened to music and opened the windows when the weather allowed. Ray Lamontagne piped through the wind of our neighborhood and became the soundtrack of many paintings. We'd take a little dance break to stretch our legs. The boys would move on from their art projects before I was done for the day, but we would check in on each other from across the room.

Callum's need for snuggles made sure I kept well within my rest limits. When 1 PM rolled around — we turned the Food Network on and snuggled on the couch. If Boston wanted to stretch out, starfish-style, he'd choose the little flip-out couch on the floor for his naptime. Through Rachael Ray and Paula Deen, the boys would rest their eyes and I'd rest my mind as the paint splatters dried on my hands.

Our Wednesday walks became Wednesday visits from Nana at my house. We'd sit in the sunroom and let the boys play. She'd scold me on days I made pumpkin muffins before she got there, but she'd eat one anyway. She'd bring coffee to me, or we'd make some at home. Strong and black for her, decaf and black for me. On days we needed new scenery, we'd go for a drive and chat about the next time we'd be walking on the riverfront.

She didn't visit us at the hospital when Beckham was born because she had a cold and was afraid she might get the baby sick, so she sent flowers in her place.

The days after Christmas are always filled with leftovers, extra sugar, lethargy, and sweatpants. It's science. Having a brand-new baby was no exception. I got a call from my Nana that she was finally feeling better, and she and Pop were coming to meet Beckham.

"Will you be ready for us at 11:00?" she asked through our phone call.

Glancing at the clock that read just after 9 — I noticed the chaos of our small home post-Christmas and newborn. The living room was filled with evidence of a newborn, including breast pads strewn about, blankets near every seat, discarded burp cloths, and unused pacifiers for a stubborn little one. Mixed in were the toddler's golf sets and books that had been abandoned, along with Snoopy plushies of all sizes, soccer balls, sippy cups, and of course, the pillow fort my oldest had made.

I couldn't bring myself to consider the dishes in the sink or cookie sheets of crumbs we had used for baking. Then I remembered the day my Nana saved me from the embarrassment of the bereavement counselor seeing my unkept house and knew she had seen me at my worst. I didn't have anything to prove to her.

"I'd love to see you!" I was excited. My mother's mother had become an integral part of our lives, something I'd missed since my Grandma Marney died.

I used the hour or so before their arrival to make pumpkin muffins (and, consequently, more mess), fix my hair a bit, and get the boys looking adorable and clean. I put on the new sweatpants my mother had gotten me for Christmas. Fancy, clean sweatpants with a logo down the leg. Comfortable and matching my house. They had a bit of flair being bright yellow. I nursed Beckham before they arrived so he could spend that time getting loved on by his great- grandmother. I never once took for granted that my children were getting time with three generations before them — something I missed out on as the youngest.

She and Great Pop came bearing Subway sandwiches. We sat and visited and talked about nothing notable as she gushed over Beckham's chubby cheeks and squishy legs. She marveled at the size of his newborn body which was closer to a 4-month-old — nearly 11 pounds at birth. She took in the improv musical performance of Boston while Callum tapped his foot in rhythm, and we talked about when we could get back to our Wednesday routine.

"Not before it warms up" she warned. I presumed this was being cautious because I had just given birth or because the boys were so young. *I have replayed this conversation a million times in my head because it was the last time my children saw her.*

Over the next couple of months, snow and freezing temperatures made it an easy decision to stay in. As the temperature began to even out and Beckham aged deeper into babyhood, I expected an invitation any day. Part of me wondered if my relationship with my Nana was slipping back to where it had been before Keely died. It had been a place we were both comfortable with until we spent time in a new place with one another.

Callum's birthday, which is at the end of April, was always a good marker for spring. I distinctly remembered watching the buds barely on the trees the day before he was born. By the time we came home from the hospital, they had been in full bloom. I also knew we'd see her around Keely's days. She would never forget. Until then, we'd keep in touch with brief phone calls and a hopeful date set for the next possibility.

My Nana didn't come to the cemetery with us that year. Though she had always come before, she said she felt a cold coming on. The wind that whipped through that part of the cemetery was particularly unforgiving, I reminded myself. The balloons flew right through Riley's tree that year. None stuck this time. Nana was tired a lot. For most 83-year-olds, that wouldn't seem out of the ordinary, but my Nana never really did get old.

I realize now that she was buying herself time to die. I believe she wanted to die without being questioned.

She had been in the hospital about a month, during the time of year that sunlight and blossoms overtake clouds and bare branches. During an evening run, without the stroller to push, I blazed past the blooming trees at lightning speed. It felt warm in the post winter Midwest as my body heated up with each mile. Then the phone rang.

It was my aunt telling me that my Nana was going to hospice. She had only been in the hospital for about a month. Nobody said it, but I already knew. I sat down on the curb to take in the information. The run that felt so fast and short just a minute ago felt heavy and unnecessary now. While still on the phone, I turned back towards home. I felt frantic — I needed to get there.

I called mom to see if she was coming. She said she planned to come tomorrow and assured me there wasn't a rush. They were just going to make her comfortable.

Once home, I filled Sam in and headed to the hospice center in my running clothes. If anyone wouldn't mind me coming to see them in my sweaty running clothes, it was my Nana.

The outside of the hospice center looked like a prison. Tall brick walls with no windows, no welcome signs, no decorations. It was much more hospitable inside. Comfortable chairs, soft music. Windows let light beam through the courtyard between the tall walls and the walls of the building. I passed it every day on the way to work for years and had no idea there was more to it than the barricade walls.

In the room, Pop sat next to her. My Nana laid there completely still with swollen fingers from all the fluids she'd been filled with at the hospital. I patted her hand and said hello softly. She looked peaceful, but not quite herself. She was still there. I knew she could hear me, but she couldn't respond.

Pop mustered up a low "A-lllly-"the way he did with every race finish line I crossed, but a whisper this time. I stayed for only a minute and let them have their time. I didn't want to intrude on those quiet moments, their last quiet moments.

I stepped out of the room and was met by my Nana's son with a notebook in hand.

"She said you knew." *Knew her final wishes* was implied. He trailed off, unable to finish the sentence.

I felt more important in that moment than I was. All those talks we had as we walked along the riverfront meant something. They weren't the same conversations she had with everyone. They were ours alone, which felt both special and heavy.

I carefully recalled what she wanted, and why it was important. *Did they need to know why? Did that matter?* It felt like information I needed

to make sure someone else knew because it was important to her —
so I shared it.

He took notes with each bullet point. Each check mark she wanted
to see was made note of. No open casket.

"Nobody needs to see my dead body." Her voice echoed in my
mind. At the time she said it, she managed for it to come off with
humor and a lighthearted air, remembering her own mother's
funeral.

There were two songs she wanted to include in the ceremony. Or, as
she said, she wanted to hear. "Because I certainly hope we can see
our own funerals. What else would they be for?" More laughter, as
it followed her always.

"The Lord's Prayer" because Frank Sinatra performed it at some
point and she worried for her relationship with God, always unsure
of if the sins of her past would haunt her.

"Annie's Song" by John Denver was the other song. She never really
told me why she chose this song, but I knew it was important to her.

Another wish of hers was not to have a viewing. It seemed
unnecessary for a woman that planned to be cremated.

"A lot of people show up to those kinds of things and have to
pretend to be sad, Aly." "I don't want that." She directed.

"Nana, I feel like those are the things that people have come to
expect and maybe even need for closure or something." I
questioned, wondering if I even believed it myself.

"Well, I guess if that's what my family wants it won't bother me."
She continued "I probably won't care." She laughed at her own joke,
thinking of herself being aggravated from the great beyond.

I leaned into her words "I guess if that's what my family wants it won't bother me."

Before I left that evening, I had a moment alone with her. Our only moment alone had been over the last four years and all in the presence of my children. Those moments were filled with grief, laughter, tears of sadness, tears of joy, stories, and memories. They had come and gone so very quickly.

In these final moments of telling her goodbye, I sang one verse of "Every Grain of Sand" very, very quietly in her ear. I know she could hear it. I could feel her hearing me. *In that moment, I felt the Master's hand.*

9

The next morning, I returned to the hospice to meet my mom and dad there. The room was packed with people. Neighbors, strangers to me, Nana's sons, their wives and families, my parents and I all stood in silence at her bedside. A priest from their church came to bless her and I remembered back to her request just a couple of weeks before.

She looked different now than she had the evening before. The swelling was gone, and she looked more like herself. Her manicured hands were back to their normal size and her rings sparkled on them like she had just finished the dishes at my grandparents' house during a family reunion. It's funny how just a glint of sparkle on a ring can bring you back in an instant to a nearly 30-year-old memory.

In those final moments with a loved one, it's easier to let yourself slide into nostalgia — to a time when an end seemed so far away, to a time when it was. The space between her breaths lengthened and, with each one, we wondered if it would be her last. The feeling I had the night before, of her being present, was no longer. She was gone already.

Pop cheered her on for one final breath as my mother's sister arrived. He wanted everyone there in time. He wanted everyone there for her. If he had a checklist, this would have been on it.

"One more breath, you can do it!" He cheered for her like she was finishing a 5K. Just a few years before, she did that exact thing and with enough breath to complain in the most hilarious way possible. It was the inspiration she needed to take that one last breath and not leave anybody with regrets.

Nobody wanted to be the first to leave the room, but the purpose of the gathering had been fulfilled.

"I'll get the nurse" her son said to no one in particular and rushed from the room. A few more people quietly made their way out. Once the nurse returned to the room to declare what we already knew, everyone silently said one last goodbye.

Mom, Dad, and I were close to the door making for an easy escape. I needed to get home to nurse my baby who would be hungry. I made plans with my parents to see them the next day when they would be in town for funeral planning. My house, filled with my babies, would be a respite from the sadness of my Nana's home. It was another time I was grateful to be in this town — to offer *something* to my mother.

The next morning, during church, I searched for a message from my Nana in the songs chosen. She wasn't there. Instead, I found God offering me just what my heart needed to hear. The sounds of my oldest son singing the handful of words in hymns he knew was what my ears needed to hear.

The weight of a permanent goodbye felt heavy, but not like the heaviness I had known before. It was tempered by knowing she had lived a long life. The burden of goodbye had been lightened by the chance to say it. Though any death is a shock, it wasn't entirely surprising when it happened. But the real shock came the day after, when grieving took hold.

After church services, we met my parents at Starbucks. It was warm outside that day, more like summer than spring. We chose to sit outside. Even though the coffee shop was next to a busy mall and busier road, the outdoor tables were fenced in. It was the perfect place to let my boys run around after being so still at church.

I enjoyed the extra-large soy latte my dad got for me when he ordered his black coffee. We nursed our drinks, waiting for the call for Mom to head to the funeral home. She had also taken notes from my discussions with my Nana on her wishes for her funeral.

My mom had wishes for her mother too. The unique situation of my mother's childhood kept her from helping plan the funeral of the woman-who-raised-her, my Marney. Now the woman she called "Mom" was ready to be laid to rest, my mom was ready to do her part.

Our drinks were already finished when my mom's phone, sitting on the iron table, began to vibrate. Before the ringtone even sounded, she answered.

My mom didn't say many words; mainly "oh" and "okay", and "hmm". Dad, Sam, and I had already started collecting our things and preparing the boys to get back in the car so Mom could get where she needed to be. She lifted her hand to us and made a motion to sit back down.

Confused, I looked to her face for more instruction and saw her eyes welling up and tears spilling down her cheeks. *Oh mama, it's becoming more real.* I looked away so she could have her privacy. I considered how selfish I'd been in my grief. Not just today, but all the time. Had I ever considered the changes my mom faced in her life? I considered it now and made a silent pledge to do so going forward.

Her goodbye to whomever was on the other end of the phone barely made a sound.

"Tuesday evening and Wednesday morning" she said to us, in a low tone. We waited for more of an explanation. It seemed strange they wouldn't be going to the funeral home to plan for a few more days.

"Why are they waiting so long to plan?" I asked, wondering if someone from out of town needed time or maybe Pop needed more time.

"No, the visitation is Tuesday. The funeral is Wednesday." She paused. "It's all done." Her voice cracked with the last words. She had been left out of planning her mother's funeral.

There were many times that my mother's unconventional upbringing made an explanation of who she was seem necessary. While she could have painted the woman-who-birthed-her-but-did-not-raise-her a villain — she defended her. She explained away that she had a blessed childhood even if her mother didn't raise her.

My mom retained gratitude for a woman who made a choice that many others found selfish. My sisters and I had the luxury of calling my Grandma Marney and my Gramps our grandparents. It simplified things. My mom called her biological mother "Mom" but that was in the title only. Once my Nana left the town she was from, she started a new life and in the very occasional times those worlds would collide, as in the case of her death — it became a gray area.

While my mother would be included in the obituary that someone else helped write, she was still considered an outsider. I will never forget the look on my mom's face that windy spring day outside Starbucks. I had seen my mom heartbroken, and in deep, inconsolable grief. I had seen her angry. I had seen her strong. I had never, though, until that afternoon seen her so devastated. Still, she wouldn't allow herself to be mad about it — just hurt.

A few days later, we were at the funeral home along with many of my mother's half and step siblings — family we only saw at funerals now. Much to our surprise, my Nana's body was there. *Not cremated.* She lay there, looking little like herself in an open casket. *All the things she decidedly did not want.* This woman spent her life doing precisely what she wanted. She made very clear her wishes for how this should all look, and here we were watching everything happen opposite her wishes.

Even though she wanted to be cremated — she hoped to not end up cremated and in the closet the way her good friend had. Her friend's husband, so proud of his frugality, bragged on the $11 vase he found at a discount home store rather than "keeping the funeral home in business", he had stated unapologetically.

"She's in a shoebox! More than 40 years married to a cheapskate, I guess she shouldn't be surprised." My Nana had laughed heartily, half certain her friend knew that's where she'd end up.

Nana had very specific plans for her burial that, should her beloved husband depart first, she'd bury him with his mother, and she would be buried with her mother. She had elaborated the 30 years she spent living with her mother-in-law was plenty long enough. If she were to go first… "Well, I guess it doesn't matter then. I doubt I'd notice."

My Nana's parents were buried just up the hill from where Keely and my Grandma Marney were buried. They rested under an 80-year-old evergreen tree that was planted in memory of Riley, my Nana's older brother who died before she was born. He was not quite 7 years old, and my Nana believed she wouldn't have been born if he'd lived. She told me how disappointed her father was that she was a girl. He never actually even alluded to it, but she could just tell in the way the baby of the family sometimes can. We laughed.

My mind went back to when she said that if she were buried where Pop decided that would be fine because these rituals are really for the living anyway. Pondering this, I looked at all the passersby of the body she didn't want anyone seeing. *This was all for them.*

I didn't think to prepare my sons to see their great Nana's body because I didn't think they would. When they saw her, I was never more grateful for their young ages than in that moment.

Callum, freshly three years old, quite certainly did not want to see her. He said "Oh no, gernana, too sleepy." He was close to saying "Great Nana" but only the closest to him knew what he meant. He chose the rapid path back to his daddy in the back of the room. I knew he didn't understand, but his adamance to get away told me maybe he understood more than I gave him credit for.

Boston wanted to see her. I told myself he didn't understand because I didn't want to have to explain. He'd been surrounded by death and grief so much in his less than six years of life. I was grateful that our Wednesdays had taken a hiatus during what turned out to be her dying. The boys remembered, but not like they might have a few months earlier. Not so abrupt. Maybe that was part of her plan.

Part of me was afraid he'd try to wake her up. My mind flipped to a wild five-year-old climbing a casket that we hadn't known would be there and then flipped back. I grabbed his hand for good measure.

I held Beckham's chubby 5-month-old thighs on one hip, and shifted my weight to support him while I held Boston's hand as we made our way to the front. I was carefully balanced in the same "funeral heels" that Mom and I had gotten at Macy's in the days after Keely died.

Pop greeted us with a "Hey, hey Al-y" the same as he did as she took her final breath. We had the usual "front of the funeral room" conversation, where I asked how he was doing, reminded him we were praying for him, and let him know we were there if he needed anything. The entire time, I could feel my son staring at the casket behind him.

This little boy had held his sister after she died. He slept through a grandparent's funeral months later. We talked about death and bereavement and hope in Christ every single day. It was genuinely a part of every single day throughout most of his life. Yet here I was afraid of what he might ask. For as much knowledge as we acquire about grieving and dying, we never really know enough.

There are still many times the right words can't be found. Maybe it's just that, at some point, we recognize that there aren't words. That seems too serious to admit to one another.

Two steps towards the casket and Boston's little voice said "Oh" softly. "It's Great Nana!" his voice cautiously cheerful. He paused.

"She's defeated." He said, not asking a question, but making a statement the way he might when a video game character dies.

I shifted the weight of Beckham and knelt to put my arm around my oldest son's shoulder. We talked about great Nana's life on earth being done. We said prayers for her health together and then prayers for her relationship with God. He knew as well as any five-year-old could know, which is probably better than a lot of adults. He didn't say much for the rest of that day —which was out of character for our talkative and rambunctious boy.

I met people on that day that I'd only heard stories of. I met many I didn't know at all, through stories, family, or otherwise. I saw strangers, acquaintances, family, and friends. I heard laughter and jokes, just as my Nana would prefer. I saw tears and heartbreak.

Though my Nana always introduced me as her granddaughter — it felt awkward to me. It was a technicality. Somewhere along the road of childhood and adolescence, it felt like a slight to my Marney — who I considered my grandmother. As my Nana and I forged a new relationship, it still felt separate and apart from her real grandchildren.

Her real grandchildren's parents were raised by her, in the same house together, and there were no alternatives that might get their feelings hurt even if they wouldn't admit it. So, when someone introduced themselves to me at my Nana's funeral, I introduced myself as "Debbie's daughter". This way, if they knew my mom, they'd know the relationship. If they didn't know my mom, they didn't need to know any more than that. Was I thinking too much about it? Probably. Was it what I felt comfortable with? Yes.

She wanted John Denver's "Annie's Song" played at her funeral. She sang it with her sisters every time the woman who would become my Nana couldn't get out of it. It always bothered her that her sister's funeral had been silent given music had been an important part of life. Growing up, they performed at many weddings of family and friends. It was the same song she had chosen to walk down the aisle to for mine and both of my sisters' weddings. On my wedding day, her son played the melody on piano as she was escorted to her seat.

To this day, I can hear those opening lines in my head when I think of her. She hadn't asked much of anyone in a long time, but this song was important to her. She never wanted anything to get too serious and the song suited her. Her grandson's guitar floated the melody through the air the day of her visitation, just as she hoped it would.

We had talked about hymns for funerals and mine would change every week with what I heard during church. So many different options. Sometimes I'd lament over not choosing other hymns for Keely's funeral. Other times, the ones we chose were just right. It was nice to talk to someone that allowed me to talk about sad things without being sad the way it's 'supposed' to look. Sadness through laughter and questions can be just what our hearts find necessary.

Nana's funeral was filled with snapshots of all the people my Nana was over her lifetime, most of which didn't overlap. She reinvented herself more than once. I volunteered to speak in honor of the relationship I had been blessed to carve out with my Nana in the four years since my daughter's death. I wanted to give my mother the space in her mother's life that she deserved. I wanted to remind people that she had a whole life before she moved away to start over and that there were residual consequences of that life that offered something beautiful and whole. I was a representative of my mom, my Marney, and the life my Nana was given at birth.

About an hour before the speaking would start, my mom asked me to come back into a little side room. This is where the kids could come to relax a little bit, have snacks, and where I could nurse. It was the room where Callum spent his time comfortably avoiding people. My mom pulled a folded piece of paper out of her purse. Her hands trembled.

My mom never cried in public. She was not a dramatic person. Most times, she was mothering someone; at least it seemed that way to me. She never asked support for anyone outside of my dad. As my sisters and I matured, we became a part of that circle of support for my mother. What an honor.

She unfolded the paper and handed it to me but held on to it too. "Would you mind reading this for me? When you go to the front?"

"You don't have to." She was talking me out of it before even letting go of the paper. "I could ask Dad to."

"Mom, I would be honored to, but you have to hand it over." I teased her to try to lighten the weight of the room. I felt so full to be able to do this for my mother. It felt like I could see in my mom, for the first time, the little girl who spent her Friday evenings sitting at the window of my grandparents' house waiting for her mother to come visit. Some weekends, she arrived. Most of the time, her arrival was in the form of a phone call and excuse. While my mother had seen past that and forged a relationship with the woman who birthed her, she remained scarred by the hurt.

I was proud of my mom for putting herself out there in words. I was proud of her for staking her claim to her mother, finally. I was proud to have the mother I did. It wasn't lost on me that I had the mother I did because of what she went through. Her hurt became our blessing.

I read through the words a few times beforehand, hopeful that I wouldn't choke on them. Dad typed it all out and printed it for her the way he had our vacation journals growing up. I knew she had a copy at home too. I kept my own words short and light, just like my relationship with my Nana had been. Short, light, and important to us both. I pulled the paper from my Bible and read my mother's words like a newscaster reporting the facts. I left no room for emotion, because I didn't want it to spill over. I had enough of crying in public and knew I wasn't primary in this grief. Sad as I may be, this storm was someone else's to weather. It was a chance to offer a bit of support back to my own mother for probably the very first time.

As I looked up from the folded paper, saying the words on it and took in the response of all the people in front of me. Some of those closest to me were experiencing their first true bout with grief. Overcome with emotion, having not faced it to this degree yet, their faces were red in anguish and cries audible. Others, perhaps even closer to her than most, had been down this road before. They'd buried parents and siblings, children even. They had accepted many years ago that death was more a part of life than most things. They had hard lessons early. Those people had become stoic, but not unscathed by repeated loss.

Pop's lighthearted demeanor was replaced with a deep, gut wrenching, palpable sadness. I stood at the front of the room with words of remembrance for his wife and with words from my mother, whose admiration stemmed from before Pop was a part of their lives. He didn't hear them. He looked down and to the side, his face drawn and sad. I could tell by his body language; he would take in none of what I was saying. He was lost in his own memories, his own broken heart. I knew no words would reach him that day.

In the four years since Keely's death, we had become well-versed in grieving for "what might have been" and all those tiny moments we missed with her, a relationship that I should have had. From that loss came a relationship with my Nana that I never thought I'd have. A gain.

Wednesdays with Nana were replaced by Wednesday morning visits from Great Pop. He had always dropped her off to us, but now he came and visited. We talked about running races and let Boston play. I made him pumpkin muffins. I found out later he never ate them. I kept making them nonetheless because I didn't want everything to be different and I think he felt the same. I think he came to our Wednesday mornings searching for her. He found his own solace in routine but it only lasted a few months. I guess he didn't find her there.

This time, unlike when my Grandma Marney died, I knew enough to be able to support my mom. It was a shift in the dynamic of our family for her to lose her mom. She still had my Gramps left, though he was in Virginia. We decided to plan a vacation to go see him. My mother and I needed a refreshed connection to the generation before her. We looked forward to a peaceful, lowkey eastern road trip. We could watch the boats on the riverfront and just sit next to him. He could tell us to "enjoy each day" and offer an occasional riddle. It was late May, and a summer trip out east would offer something to look forward to all of us. The big boys had gotten to know Gramps in person already from visits, but Beckham at his ripe age of six months hadn't yet. We were due for a visit.

10

"Hello?"

"Hey babe. Sorry to bother you while you're getting ready for church." My mom was on the other end of the phone. Her words were casual, but her tone was shaky. I knew something was wrong.

Just six weeks had passed since we stood in the room full of people waiting for my Nana to take her last breath. Now we had gotten the call that my Gramps died in his sleep the night before. We didn't get to say goodbye. It had been a gift we had gotten used to — the extra chance to say anything you needed to say. But just like when he left us before, he wouldn't face the finality of goodbye.

We started preparations to head there, not knowing many details. The information from Gramps' niece who lived near him was limited at best, and we didn't want to intrude too much as she was burdened with the arrangements.

Each day that passed after hearing the news we figured we'd know something soon. He was having a military funeral so maybe it took longer to organize. We questioned. Finally, a few days later we got more information. They were burying him in two hours. His niece said he didn't want people there. *People. We weren't people, we were family.* He'd be buried with military honors, laid to rest alongside his brothers in arms. *Without us present.*

I didn't see my mom's face as she relayed this information to me because we were on the phone, but I would imagine it looked very similar to the face I had seen at Starbucks six weeks before. Part of me was glad I wasn't seeing it again, but a bigger part of me wished

I could have given her a hug at that moment. I found no words because there were none.

"I'm sorry, mom." I didn't know what else to say.

"I know babe. I'm sorry for you too." She answered softly.

And with that, we went on with our day as normal. Meanwhile, a 21-gun salute sounded halfway across the country for the man that raised my mother and the man I called my Grandpa. We never really got to say goodbye — not the way we wanted to say goodbye, at least.

***

Five years after his beloved wife left this earth, while I was still a young teenager, my Gramps left Indiana. He headed back to Virginia to familiarity. He headed back to be near his brother. He headed back to watch the boats on the river he'd watched as a young boy. One day, he just left.

I never really believed he'd leave. I only knew him as my grandpa — I never considered his childhood with six siblings. Or how his time in the Marine Corps was more than me trying on his uniform hat occasionally or hearing the story of how he met my grandmother in the service shaped him. I didn't consider that he had a life anywhere but where I was.

Truly though, before he left, I had left him. I left him for adolescent things. I left him for movies and slumber parties and soccer games. I left my Gramps to grow up and he was leaving now to reconnect to his youth. A weird crossroads.

The walk I took in my jelly shoes a few years before had become my peaceful, quiet, alone time, walking between my house and my grandparents' house. Most days of the year, I took those walks to pray or sing loud or just listen. The jelly shoes were replaced with decidedly teenage sandals and soccer cleats. If I stayed too late and it was dark, my dad would pick me up in his little jeep and we'd drive through the field.

As I got deeper into the double digits, I spent less time managing the pool. I visited the kitties less and less. I started going to the movies with friends, school dances, and birthday parties more and more. I did all the things a little girl does less and less, including spending time with my Gramps.

I wish now I'd kept asking him to play Go Fish and Boggle on Sundays or make sure there were still kitties in the barn. *Where did they all go?* Sundays often left us heading home earlier than we used to, even my mom. My sisters and I would fight over the phone, like we did every other day. My aunt would work on Sunday afternoons and my Gramps would sleep in front of the tv with football on. He'd do so unbothered, but alone. Always alone.

The morning he was to leave, my mom left our house before anybody else was awake. He was leaving at 8 AM and she was going to help pack his car and wave goodbye. She pulled through the field that separated our houses and his station wagon was already gone. He couldn't bear to say goodbye face to face, so he had already left.

I was planning to say goodbye later in the morning, so I still wasn't dressed when my mom came back in. I stood in the kitchen in my pajamas with puffy morning eyes and unkempt hair that became curly and unruly in puberty. Mom's eyes were red. She told me he was gone in a way that I didn't want to ask more.

Once he settled in Virginia, I would go as a teenager, a visitor. I would go as a decidedly different person- a taller, older, more mature person. I stayed mad for a little while. I was mad that he left. I was mad that he didn't say goodbye. I was mad that he only came back a few times. I was mad that he spent so much time with his high school sweetheart, who was alone again after her husband died. If it had been a story I read in a newspaper "Man and high school sweetheart reunite to keep each other company in their old age", I would've thought how nice that was. I would've thought it was wonderful that they had something kind of familiar so they wouldn't be lonely. I would've thought they could grieve together, maybe even heal a little. I would've seen God's hand if it were strangers. But I didn't. I was mad that he didn't stay in grief for my grandmother.

I saw Virginia as the place that took my Gramps away, but it was the place that gave him life both in the beginning and at the end. Only now do I understand that he did stay in grief for my grandmother, which is why he had to go back to the only place he'd known without her.

As I've let my anger dissipate and have matured, I've started to accept grief like glitter in a classroom. Once it's there, it's always there. It pops up in surprising places; sometimes a little, sometimes a lot. You can go awhile without noticing it, but then there's a twinkle here or sparkle there. It wasn't a heavy or deep realization for me. It was logical. I know I'll be okay and then I won't be okay, but I'll be okay again. A simplified kid version of grieving? Yes. A version I still call on as an adult —absolutely. Sometimes we adults overcomplicate things.

I continued taking care of the cemetery alone. It had been my "job" with my Gramps when my grandmother Marney died, and I kept it up after he moved away. It felt like a visit with both of my grandparents even though one was still alive. Those tiny purple crocuses offered a friendly "hello".

My mom would drive me there and wait in the car. I think she knew I wanted to be alone out there, and I think she didn't want to be there, but knew I needed it. The wind always howled on the hill at the cemetery where generations of my family were laid to rest. I listened to the chimes we set out for my grandmother. I listened to the whistling tree but stopped whistling back — that was only when Gramps was there. I decorated it with little angels that were often stolen. My mother told me if someone stole an angel from a cemetery, they probably needed it more than we did. I suppose that's true.

Eventually I could drive myself to the cemetery, in the same blue truck that belonged to my Gramps. He left it for me. My mother was relieved she didn't have to go so much, and I was happy to go alone. Rather than the manager of the pool, I was the manager of the graves at the cemetery. My name was never on the sign, but the role continued anyway.

When I wasn't tending to graves at the cemetery like any normal 15-year-old — I took to my sketchbook. I spent hours drawing angels and heavenly things. It was easy because nobody really knew what they looked like, so my artistic privilege meant I was never wrong. I obsessed over the eyes in any drawing. They needed to be perfect and never quite were. The light, the shadows, the weight of faces in each line of charcoal or lead was stressed and refined. I found a lot of healing in those lines.

My quiet walks down the hill stopped altogether when Gramps moved away. We continued Sunday dinners for a while, maybe in hopes of holding on to something we knew my grandparents wanted us to —but it wasn't there.

Behind those flannel shirts and JNCO jeans, my mind was maturing faster than my wardrobe. I began going to the Bible directly for answers. I dug through the pages of my baby blue Precious Moments Bible and cringed at the misspelling of my sister's name in the front. I had written the date of her baptism in the records in dark blue pen, then scribbled it out and re-wrote it correctly. Nobody would notice, I'm sure. So much for my career in calligraphy.

I made little hearts and cross references. I started to think of *forever.* The first time I considered baptism, I remembered holding my middle sister's electric blue Debbie Gibson hat and purple blazer that I'd held as she was baptized. She was the first person to be baptized in the baptistry that was hidden under the pulpit most of the time — it was a new addition to the building. Before then, members of the church were baptized in the river, or they'd borrow the baptistry of another congregation.

My middle sister seemed more grown up at her baptism than I felt now — a few years later. I hadn't done anything *that* bad, I thought to myself. I also didn't know what I was waiting for — I didn't have any big plans for sin either. One spring afternoon, I came home from school and took my shoes off to walk through the yard. I picked two dandelions with my backpack still filled with schoolbooks on my shoulders. As I walked to the door of my home, I twisted the dandelion stems together tucked them into the collar of our chunky Australian Shepherd, Winnie. Before I even dropped my bookbag on the floor, I blurted out "I want to get baptized" to my mom. Then I continued up the stairs to my room.

Not long later, I saw my dad driving up the quarter mile driveway like there was a bee in the car. My parents were as ready as I was.

We drove to the little country church that was our home church. It was the same church my dad stood at the front and preached at every Sunday. No one had been baptized there since my sister. The iron handle that led to the front door was the same one I flipped over after services as a young kid. I was probably swinging on it when some elderly church member needed it to steady themselves, but nobody ever mentioned it.

The iron handle shook a bit when I took hold of it, or maybe it was my hands. The door opened, and the afternoon light danced through the windows. They looked like broken pieces of frosted glass all stuffed into a frame of unbroken glass. You couldn't see through them, and they didn't offer much light on a typical day. This day was different as the light beamed through them in a new way.

It was my turn to wear the all-white outfit. My mom laid towels out leading from the baptistry to the classrooms in the front of the church. The air filled with the smell of chlorine with the baptistry open. My dad wore waders like he was going fishing. On the way to the church, I briefly considered how cool it would have been to be baptized in the river.

When the cold water of the indoor baptistry hit my body — I was glad it wasn't the April waters of the river. As I answered the question with "Yes, I believe Jesus is the son of God" and became fully submerged in the water, I opened my eyes. Through the clear water, the broken afternoon light danced with sun, with luminosity, with hallelujah.

I created a painting of all blues, all shades, all joy, all light, and all mine from that day. Nobody else could ever know what that painting, what those colors, and that moment meant to me. It's all mine, just like my walks with God.

I rode home from the church that day unafraid of a car accident. I continue my life unafraid most of the time, knowing I will never be alone. Though life tests my confidence — He is always good.

My dandelions were still twisted into my dog's collar when we got home. I took them off her, told her how cute she was, and offered her a favorite treat —bread —for keeping my treasure safe. I pressed the twisted flowers into a book and stuck it back onto the shelf.

Life continued, mostly normal, but better, clearer, and with more sun. *How could there be more sun than what I had?* I found out when I opened my eyes under the waters of baptism.

***

After hearing the news of my Gramps' passing and of his already-happened funeral, we switched from planning a road trip to visit him to a week at the beach — my mother's happy place. My dad's trusty gold atlas would get us anywhere. Listening to the waves crash, feeling the hot sand, watching the sun rise and fall each day felt like the perfect therapy to allow Mom to grieve. The beach was the only vacation spot my mom was picky.

If you said we were going to the beach, you'd better be able to touch the sand, hear the surf, and watch the waves right from your balcony. I learned very young the differences between beach front, beachside, near the beach, view of the beach, waterfront, or sea wall. For my mom, it was beach front all the way. It was the only time my mom was a morning person. She didn't want to miss a minute of the ocean. It was the perfect escape.

Being the planner that I am, changing a vacation destination just a few weeks before felt very spontaneous — I hated it. But it was exactly the distraction that my mom needed. Finding two beach front suites side by side that fit our growing family plus mom and dad felt like we won the lottery — especially in July.

Due to the abbreviated planning time, each day in preparation was filled with excitement and list-making. I packed for the little boys and myself. Sam was on his own — he'd wait until the very last minute anyway.

Before I knew it, we were on the road for the 12-hour car trip that ended up taking 14 or 15 with stops for nursing and diaper changes. Kids' music filled the air with songs and mysteries and repetition. I sat in the back, keeping the baby boys entertained unless Sam needed help navigating. Little snacks and riddle games made the hours pass quickly while naps worked like magic.

It felt like not much time had passed since vacations on the road were spent in the back of my parents' gray van. The bench seat farthest in the back laid all the way down to create a full-sized bed. For long trips, my mom covered it in a fitted sheet so she could easily clean the crumbs out before hitting the road every morning. During the day, it was my domain. Relegated to the back seat by being the baby and being one of the few to not get car sick — it was my kingdom. I always brought too many Barbie dolls and baby dolls. These were the same dolls I stuffed into cannons at Gettysburg for a picture and gave a beach wedding to in Florida. Now, here I was, in the backseat of our much-smaller-than-a-full-size-van-SUV with my three boys — doling out snacks, playing with action figures, and changing out batteries in electronics to keep the boys occupied. The feeling of excitement remained.

We met up with Mom and Dad somewhere along the route and took pictures of each other's cars in excitement. We pulled in while the sun was past its peak for the day. The purples and oranges of the falling rays lit up the sand not long after we arrived. We let the boys dance at the edge of the ocean, getting sand and water all over their clothes and allowing their legs to stretch and recover from the long drive. I was tired from the ride and from the events of the last couple of months. I expected the same of Mom, but she was invigorated by her happy place. She was high from the smell of salt water and the heat of the sand on her feet.

This is just what she needed. I fought off the urge to rush everyone into jammies so I could put my feet up. Instead, I took those moments in —the way moments are meant to be savored.

Years before, I had read about the Kennedy family finding solace in the sea after one of their untimely deaths. Here I was, witnessing that very thing in person, in the form of my mother's healing heart. A weight was lifted the second we stepped out onto the falling tide. We stayed on the beach until the night had claimed anything we could see with our bare eyes. We were exhausted and hungry but unwilling to leave this moment any earlier than necessary.

When we finally headed up to our suites, pants sticky with sand and salt water, Sam and Dad left to pick up dinner and bring it back. Before they even returned, my little boys were bathed and jammied, with Beckham asleep for the night and Callum close behind. We forced him to eat a little bit of food in his jammies before letting him pass out next to his big brother, who felt like a king for being allowed to eat dinner on a tray in bed while watching cartoons. It was everything a vacation should be.

As the children drifted off to sleep one by one, I could take a deep breath and relax in a different way. Beckham slept in the crook of my left arm, as I ate my Thai noodles with my right. When I finished my dinner, I carried Beckham onto the balcony and got comfortable by tucking pillows around my arms. Sam brought me a black coffee and Mom brought her chair out too.

Glancing at the dark swirls of bubbles and dark liquid in the hotel room mug, I thought of my Nana. It didn't feel like all that long ago that I was downing this very drink on a walk along the riverfront with her. I knew she was on Mom's mind too as the ocean was one thing the two women had in common. Gramps had moved back to his first home to watch the boats on the water, so his memory haunted us that evening too. They were on our hearts.

The night was dark, but the moon lit the waves up in the ocean just enough to see the tide shift. The lights were on in the pool three stories below us. Teenagers played like little kids in the green underwater lights, laughing and splashing at one another.

As Mom sat down, she patted my leg. "I sure am glad you're here with us, Babe." She said, calling me by the same pet name she used for all three of her daughters.

"I'm glad we could be here, Mom. Are you doing okay?" I knew that she'd say whatever she thought I needed to hear, but I'd read between the lines.

"Well," she sighed deeply. "I don't know."

She continued after a long pause. "I think so."

The fizz of her diet coke opening broke the silence that only lingered between waves crashing. The air felt lighter.

We listened to the teenagers continue their games.

"Do you think they are brothers and sisters?" I asked, knowing we were both listening to the same thing.

"Maybe." Mom considered "Maybe cousins." We laughed that they were probably cousins because of how well they were getting along. Though who was closest shifted from time to time, Mom and Dad's grandchildren all seemed to enjoy their time with one another. Mom and Dad enjoyed nothing more than seeing that.

"Do you think we'll get everybody here at the same time?" I asked Mom, knowing it was what she wanted most.

"Well, probably not, but wouldn't that be nice?" Her eyes sparkled with enthusiasm.

We calculated Mom and Dad's 45th anniversary would be three years away. I knew that Sam and I weren't done having children. We had a new baby every two and a half years, so if everything went as it had been going, we'd be having a baby that year. Maybe their 50th anniversary made more sense, we decided.

"Wouldn't it be special to have all of my grandchildren here together for our anniversary?" She glowed. "The trip of a lifetime!".

"Almost all of them." She patted my leg, letting me know she remembered.

We pondered if the two future children Sam and I hoped to have would be girls or boys. We considered how old Keely would be if she were alive. *What time of the year would make it easiest for everyone? Could we talk my brothers-in-law into it?* We thought of all the roadblocks and how to get around them. Our conversation kept our hearts full for hours that night and I left on a mission to talk my sisters into helping me plan. We had eight years. It should be enough, even though it was a tall order. I like a challenge and a vacation.

We sat on that balcony well past Beckham's midnight feeding and eventually the travel of the day caught up to me. By the time my eyelids were heavy, the teenagers were long gone from their night in the pool. The silence of the night was punctuated only by the soothing breaking of waves.

Mom moved her chair so I could easily navigate carrying my very large seven-month-old into his bed. As she got up, she gave me a kiss and repeated her earlier sentiment "I'm so glad you guys are here."

"Me too, Mom. Good night." I couldn't hug her with my hands full, so I laid my head on top of hers. She was short enough — it was an easy feat. She patted Beckham's chubby cheeks as we made our way past her. As I got situated in bed, I could hear her chair adjust. She'd stay out there just a little while longer.

***

The smell of coffee hung in the hotel room as I awoke. I was eleven years old and on vacation with my parents and middle sister. My oldest sister had finally talked mom and dad into letting her stay home, much to my mom's disappointment. The door to the balcony was cracked open with one of my dad's loafers wedged in it, and the sounds of ocean waves were only broken by the crinkling of my dad's newspaper. My middle sister was still asleep next to me, my mom nowhere to be seen. The sun was starting to peek over the horizon.

"Good morning, Dad" I said with a stretch and a yawn.

"Hey Chooch", Dad responded as one side of the newspaper folded over while he took a sip of coffee.

"Is Mom gone already?"

114

"She'll be back soon. Have a danish." He said, nodding to a paper plate of donuts from the complimentary breakfast.

So fancy – a regular donut with what might have been classified as fruit and a sprinkling of icing. It seemed like something Princess Diana might have for breakfast. I thought about this as I took my pastry onto the balcony. I carefully stepped over the shoe keeping the door ajar.

It was humid already and the curls around the nape of my neck didn't take long to spring. I sat in my nightgown on the metal deck chair and looked across the beach for mom. I saw a runner and an elderly couple but couldn't find mom. After a while, a young man that worked for the hotel started carrying out umbrellas and wedging them into the sand one by one, slowly, like he was getting paid by the hour. I finally spotted Mom. She was walking right along the shoreline; she'd stop to touch a shell with her toe. If it met her search criteria (I never knew what that was), she'd reach down and put it in the cup she carried with her. She went a few paces and stopped again, resting her hands on her hips. This time, maybe just to look out at the ships far off the shore or take a deep breath.

I fought the urge to call out to her because it felt early, and I might have been too far away for her to hear me. Even so, it felt like I was witnessing a private moment of hers, and I didn't want to intrude. On the beach, my mom was both a morning person and a night person. She didn't want to waste one single second of that salty air.

***

Now I had grown out of my adoration of Danish pastries, but my mom never outgrew the peace she found on the beach. As the sun rose the morning after we began planning the 50th anniversary party, I walked the shoreline with my chubby baby on my hip. Mom walked along the edge of the water each day we spent at the beach, but she was usually alone. We gave her space and meandered our own way. It was crisp for a summer morning and my arms chilled. I stuck my feet into the rising tide and let them sink into the sand. The sand that was so light and airy a few feet away sucked my toes down deeper into the earth. As a kid, I would wait until I couldn't stand it anymore. I pictured it up to my knees like quicksand in the cartoons. I liked to wait until it felt urgent. Then I'd wiggle my toes loose to allow the water to wash sand away, freeing my feet.

There's something about a peaceful oceanside morning that seems *emotional.* The sounds of rushing waters around you and an occasional chirp of a seagull, the grains of sand sneaking in between your toes as the tide swells, the smell of salt hanging in the air — overwhelming my senses. As I pushed the sand around with my toes while my baby curled onto my shoulder, I took in every sensation.

It isn't unlike grief, is it?

My mind conjures up an image of grief in physical form. I picture someone laying in the sand as the tide rises, letting your body sink into the earth. With each rolling wave, you gasp for a breath just in time for the water to cover your mouth and nose once again. You'd have to hold on until another chance to breathe came along. It might seem like hours when only seconds have passed. Just when you think you have a pattern figured out, a larger wave crashes around you.

Other beachgoers watch and wonder. They might ask if you're okay or if you need help, but never really offer any because they aren't sure what to do themselves, so you become banter for the rest of their stroll.

As the water rises, the weight of the sand grips your limbs, making them heavy; eventually immobile. Your breaths struggle to sustain you. Between waves, you can hear the commentary from the shore.

"That's not what drowning looks like." I imagine their observations, within earshot but not to help. "She should just get up." Everybody there knows what drowning looks like. They've read about it, they've seen it in movies, maybe even been there themselves. "Why doesn't she get up? That's what I do." Everyone is so sure of the answers when they aren't the ones in the water.

"You should scream!" Someone calls out. "She should scream if she's drowning. She's too calm." They whisper to one another. They quietly correct and judge. "You're doing it wrong!" They offer unsolicited advice, but never an outstretched hand.

They'll tell people walking by. "I was there! I saw the whole thing- it was so bizarre." They'll offer perspective and commentary while a quiet drowning isn't quite finished yet.

That's grief, I thought to myself as I snapped back to the reality of my senses filled with salt water and sand. There's one way to do grief – their way. That's the right way to drown.

If only that were true. When you're the one underwater, you're only thinking about survival, not how it looks to those on the safety of the shore.

I played this ridiculous story out as the sun started to turn hot for the day and I traced my toes in the peaceful shoreline. I laughed to myself.
Then I looked around and wondered if the few people out on the sand right now at the break of day were also searching for their footing in grief.

They were spotted figures, dotting the landscape of an early morning vacation spot. I couldn't see their faces from where I stood, we were all spaced too far away. *A handful of drowning people — all on land.*

11

Just after returning from the beach, Sam and I found ourselves putting down new roots in a new town a few hours away. We left behind the house our sons came home from the hospital to — the house Keely was alive in. We left the house Nana had visited. We also left behind the hospital the kids were born in — the same one Keely died in. It was the right move for several reasons, but the timing felt heavy. We had to lean into God's understanding, and trust. His timing is perfect.

We also left behind the doctors and nurses we trusted and who had comforted us in our darkest hour. This realization repeated through my anxious mind often as we prepared to move.

We searched high and low for the perfect home in the perfect school district. We never quite found what we were looking for, so we built it instead. Our home overlooked rolling hills of horse fields that glowed yellow in the evenings against a west facing sky. We planted a weeping cherry blossom tree for Keely. We bought birdseed and butterfly statues for it —something tangible we could do for her.

As it all lined up, we were set to move into the house in May and our fifth baby was due in July. It would be the perfect timing to get settled and bring the baby home to our new house.

The new doctors seemed…fine. I had grown so attached to our doctor who wore Christmas present earrings in the delivery room. She was no nonsense and didn't sugarcoat a word, which I loved and appreciated.

She cried with us as we watched Keely's heart stop. She repeated how special it was that we had that moment. She was just as relieved as us when Callum took his first breath. These new doctors weren't her.

Not only that, but the new medical care team didn't seem to know me or *care* all that much about getting to know me. I saw different doctors every visit. Each one would have me repeat my medical history. They would repeat back to me "stillbirth" with no emotion behind it. *She was more than that.* Maybe it was because they had so many patients that they were overwhelmed. Maybe it was because it was my fifth child, so they thought I didn't need much guidance. Whatever the reason, the nerves I felt never really felt quenched by a visit the way they had with my other doctor. When I left my doctor's appointments in our old town, I was filled with relief that would dissipate as time ticked farther from seeing the flickering heartbeat.

Though these doctors did all the same things, they weren't the same ones that had been in the ultrasound room with us. They weren't the doctors that held Keely's tiny body and allowed only a few tears to fall. They weren't the doctors whose faces filled with compassion in the silence after delivery. They weren't *our* doctors. They had an impossible task — to make me feel safe.

I worried my anxious feelings were a bad premonition. It is so easy to mistake fear with intuition and believe something bad is going to happen. My motherly instincts were on overdrive and often — thanks to God— wrong. I never felt like I could trust a good feeling, so I focused on the negative ones.

Despite the fear and worry, I was also filled with excitement and anticipation. I planned for the baby and planned for the house. One new thing with this doctor was the bloodwork that was available now, relatively early on, which meant we found out the sex of the baby much sooner than before.

During this time, the dates for our house got pushed back, but construction had barely started. I am usually a lover of a winter with heavy snow, but not when a house is supposed to be built.

One afternoon, I was expecting a phone call needing more unexpected cash from the contractor or a date delay when my phone started ringing as I pulled into the parking lot of an outlet mall. Boston was at school, and I had Callum and Beckham with me. I turned and shhhh'd them with a finger over my lips as I prepared to answer the phone, hoping they'd be quiet.

"Mrs. Elliott?" the woman on the other end of the line asked.

"It is." I responded, steadying myself for whatever bad construction news they were about to give me.

"I'm calling from the doctor's office. I have the results of your bloodwork." She paused for what seemed like 400 years.

"Yes?" I was suddenly paralyzed in fear. I had been so focused on a girl or boy, *had I forgotten to pray for health? What kind of mother would forget?* I couldn't remember at that moment.

"Everything looks great. All your levels are normal. Baby looks healthy." She went on. "Would you like to know the sex?" She doublechecked.

My heart was beating a thousand miles a minute and from the middle of my throat,

"Yes, please." I started crying before she even answered.

"You're having a girl." She sounded so certain.

"Are you sure?" Did I hear it right? I asked myself questions too.

"Yes, it's a girl, Mrs. Elliott."

"Okay, thank you." I said through unhidden tears and a shaking voice as we hung up the phone.

With hands trembling, I typed out the words to text Sam — then deleted it. I couldn't text this. I also couldn't drive an hour away to tell him in person. I certainly couldn't *wait* until he was home that evening to tell him. It was more likely that I'd fly to his work to tell him rather than wait.

I deleted my original text, tears down my face, and put in all capital letters…CALL ME. Looking back, I maybe should've added some context to a text from a pregnant wife with young children. But he called immediately, so maybe not.

There were a lot of long pauses on that phone call as we considered what this meant for our family. We'd been a family with living boys for a long time now. We were comfortable with living sons and remembering our daughter. *What would this look like?*

She said the baby was healthy, but I was too scared to believe it. Nonetheless, when Sam had to get back to his job and off the phone, we ran into the store with just enough time before Boston's school bell would ring to pick up a pink girly sleeper for a newborn baby.

She would be named after my grandmother, though she would have her own spelling: Marnie. I liked that the spelling made it mean "of the sea".

We adjusted to the idea of having another daughter; a living sister for the boys, a girl whose big sister could never braid her hair or pick out her outfits. I knew, for sure, that we couldn't be done having children now. At least one more after this. I didn't want our sons to think we were trying until we got a girl, and I didn't want our daughter to think she was a replacement for her older sister. I just wanted them all to know how deeply we loved them, and how infinitely blessed I am to be their mother.

Mom's visits turned into pink and ruffly shopping sprees, as we prepared the big brothers and planned for the house. The dates started looming suspiciously close to one another. Would the baby or the house be ready first?

We enjoyed being in the same town as one of my sisters for the first time in 10 years. We met at the park weekly for the kids to play with their cousins. We were at the park the day before my induction date when my water broke. Surprise, Marnie wanted to pick her own birthday! She almost made it the next day because she took her sweet time being born.

I had plenty of time to read the Bible this time, over and over and time to pray that this daughter could look us back in the eyes. Delivery was smooth and easy, and we brought our living daughter Marnie home to the house that was finished about ten days beforehand. Just in time— God's perfect timing.

We began to settle in again, realizing that "settling in" is just a part of being a grown up. How exhausting. We settled into our new home with our four living children, among the memory of our oldest daughter. Life felt like a sigh of relief.

The boys were instantly protective big brothers. I loved watching them in total comfort in this home, making their rooms their own special places, and making sure they were close to one another. Beckham chose a fox comforter for his bed, Callum chose soccer, and Boston chose dinosaurs. These were the places that would be the backdrop for the childhood memories they'd call on as adults.

We put roots down that Sam never got to experience himself but was able to give his kids. We were able to breathe after holding our breath for so long.

We'd been busy; busy grieving, busy moving forward, busy raising small children, busy with a still-new business. Busy and blessed. It was a golden era and every sunset falling across the horse field was a reminder to have gratitude to God for giving us these blissful moments. I never once took for granted that sweet season.

Less than two years later, we were expecting again. This time, without the chaos. We were settled and secure. We had living boys and a living girl. We had a house filled with memories and more to come. Each Christmas, their matching stockings would be lined up on the same mantle. Each Easter brought bunny eggs into the same yard. Each summer was filled with splashes into the same pool. We knew where we'd be a year from now, five years from now, ten years from now. This was more ready than we could have ever imagined. This child would be the final puzzle piece. This child would be our deep breath of fresh air.

I was just a couple of months pregnant when we found out we were having a third girl. Three girls and three boys. Perfect.

Around the same time, I successfully talked Sam into homeschooling the kids. It wasn't one big event or happening that made the decision for us, but a million little nudges that led us to that decision.

Much to Callum's dismay, our two oldest boys would finish out their third and first grade school years. We leaned into God's direction and let Him show us the way. The golden era continued. Everything was perfect, which I'm always a little suspicious of. We rode out my morning sickness in the pool. Who would've thought the best relief was the pool? But it was.

My photography work at the studio was steady and fulfilling. I went into my studio on the town square several days a week when Sam was finished with work for the day. He had a new job at this time and happened to be about a block away from my studio. The hours were more predictable. Our weekends were now untouched by his work and shifted to filling sessions for my work. We couldn't have planned it better. The kids and I could meet Sam at lunch breaks for me to have a quick meeting if the evenings were too full.

Our youngest daughter was due to arrive in January. My mom would tease us for years that we should name a baby after her. I teased her back that we were going to name it "Big Baby Elliott" in honor of my mom. My usually reserved mother would howl with laughter at that and tell her friends on their lunch dates.

I'll never be sure if Mom was surprised or not when we told her that we were, in fact, naming the baby after her. Rather than "Big Baby", the baby would be "August Debra", sharing the name Debra with my mom. We'd call her AD, which soon morphed into "ADbug" then "ADbug ladybug" even before she was born.

"You guys really don't have to do that." My mom said, choking up. "I know, Mom. We want to."

"Well, my…" she continued "What an honor". My mother was always happy to be in the cheering section of sports and of life. She didn't need the spotlight and didn't particularly want it.

This one time, though, she gladly accepted the honor. She got her youngest grandchild's name embroidered on anything that would hold the thread.

We kicked off our homeschooling journey in the fall and by the holidays we had found our rhythm. We enjoyed more time at home throughout Thanksgiving and Christmas. We baked cookies, watched every holiday movie we could, and failed miserably at building a gingerbread house.

After the holidays, we settled in barely long enough to catch our collective breath before August Debra arrived. In very late January, after 52 long hours of labor, our 10 lb queen was born just after noon. She had cheeks for miles, and we were more than ready to get back home with our family, as whole as it could be on earth.

Knowing she was our last child, I kept thinking how I wanted just one image of all six of them together. How could I make that happen? My heart broke when I really thought about it. Then the wheels of creativity started churning. *She is with them, and us, but nobody*

We created "52 week project" of images with every child's birth. They were one family picture every week of all of us. We included Keely in different ways each week. We created her name with branches of trees, made a heart of clouds in the sky, held her blanket from the hospital, snuggled a teddy bear of hers. We held up a picture of her and stood next to graffiti about love. We had dozens and dozens of ways we had included her yet none of them felt complete the way my heart needed them to.

I began to develop a concept, then sketches, of an idea that I was still working the details out of in my head.

"Would this be weird?" I asked my husband. It was a conversation we had a million times before. He and I met as art majors in college. Though he had gone back for a degree in technology, he still had an artist's spirit. I took full advantage of having another creative mind in my home —especially because he didn't sugarcoat his critique. He was my greatest asset. This question still got his attention.

Sometimes the answer was yes. Sometimes the answer was yes, but in a good way. Sometimes the answer was no, not at all. Sometimes he needed more information.

"What if I created an image of Keely with the rest of the kids, but she was in a reflection?" I held my breath.

I knew that describing something wasn't as effective as showing him, but I only had words so far. I'd need his help creating the rest.

After a long pause and a little bit of a nose scrunch that he thought I wouldn't detect, he responded "Well, yeah. It does sound weird."

I waited for the obligatory "but in a good way", but it wasn't coming this time.

"Sorry, babe." He was always more delicate where Keely was involved. He was that way with his daughters.

I was annoyed but appreciative. I was also unmoved. The more I considered it, the more I needed to see it through. Worst case scenario was that it was, in fact, a terrible idea. Even if that were the case, nobody else would even need to know.

"Would you still help me with it?" I asked him.

"Of course." He answered, both of us knowing what his answer to that would be. His analytical mind couldn't picture it quite yet, but he trusted me especially when it came to our kids.

12

One week after AD was born, Mom and I spent a few hours taking photos at my studio of our newest not-so-little bundle of joy, and everybody else came later for a few family images.

I was without makeup — not feeling like myself at all — but I followed my own advice and got in the pictures. I even talked my photo-averse mom into getting into a portrait with her namesake. It didn't even take much convincing, as Mom was a softy when it came to the grandkids. I was happy that we were able to get a picture all together. *I didn't realize at the time how I would cherish these photographs in the years to come.*

That evening, I felt the familiar pangs of a breast infection coming on. As an over-lactating mother, I recognized quickly when something was off. As the evening progressed, I knew the best course of action was to nurse, nurse, nurse as often as I could and to try to rest.

The next day I spent cozy on the couch with my kids playing around me. We did schoolwork in the living room and used some documentaries to pass the time

That evening, I took my temperature. Staying steady. August slept in my arms, as she had the whole day. This time, her arm was out to the side. So, I did what any mother would do and took her temperature. I was in disbelief as the numbers ticked up higher and higher then into triple digits. It kept going. I felt her head. She didn't feel hot.

"Sam! Come here. Feel her head." I called to my husband. He rushed over, hearing the urgency in my voice.

"She feels fine." He responded, a man very used to my sometimes overreacting to our children's medical needs.

I held up the thermometer that had finally come to a stop and beeped. His face held the same confusion as mine.

"Is that from her?".

"Yes".

Panic started creeping into my voice, but not without confusion. She felt fine. She looked fine. She acted fine. I had only taken her temperature because I was sick. I was sick. Not my baby. She couldn't be.

I took it again, thinking it had been a glitch in the thermometer. Same reading. A third and fourth time with a different thermometer rendered the same results.

I called the pediatrician after hours number. *Why do these scares always happen after dark? Why is everything scarier when the sun is down?* The nurse told me to bring her in to be seen immediately.

We loaded the kids into the car. My hands shook as I buckled the car seat on our youngest child.

Though they weren't sure what the problem was, given she was only a few days old, we were sent to the hospital for the night.

A week after giving birth, my hormones were every which way. Tears came easily and quickly. When they said our other children couldn't stay, my heart just couldn't take it. Sam kept me calm.

"It's just a night." His hands on my shoulders were strong and reassuring. "One night. No big deal."

He assured me he'd take the kids back to the house and they'd sleep and be right back to us first thing in the morning. I kissed my other kids on the head and asked them to take care of each other. I told them I'd see them in a couple of hours. The countdown began for me before they were even at the elevator. Sam and I traded phones because while I had thought to grab my Bible, I hadn't thought to grab a phone charger.

The hours stopped moving. With Sam's phone in hand, I called to tell my parents what was happening. Sam had already let them know. I was glad to be able to say less words. They, too, reassured me.

Being forced away from most of my family for the night, I felt so alone. I took turns flipping through the Bible, searching for a sign. AD rested comfortably in my left arm and nursed when she stirred even a little.

The only reason I took her temperature that night was because I was sick. She looked and felt fine. The only reason I took her temperature was because I was *led to*. It felt like divine intervention. It felt like the hand of the Holy Spirit himself had moved her arm and put it on my heart to check for a fever. Maybe that was saving her. I searched the Bible for something to ease my heart or occupy my mind. I kept turning back to Isaiah 41:10. I zeroed in on the words "I will help you."

"I will help you." I repeated the words to myself over and over that night. Words straight from God to my heart. I will help you.

I traced her fat cheeks with my fingers and wiped my tears from them.

The nurses checked on her each hour. Everything was good. The mystery seemed far less scary because she looked so good. But that scared me too. How would I know if something was getting worse?

I was relieved to be in the hospital, but desperate for my family to be with me. The night was long.

By the time morning visiting hours arrived, her temperature had fallen. It wasn't gone, but it was lower. That seemed like a win to me, but her doctors were not convinced. They seemed confused. At one point early in the day, I watched a doctor do the same google search I had done on repeat. I looked at her, then at the screen, then at her. I searched for some reassurance that she had more information than I had, myself being an artist and not a doctor. Same google results. Hmm.

Lie to me I told her from my own thoughts. It made my hands shake more.

When Sam and the kids returned, I felt relieved. I knew the moment I saw Marnie that Daddy let her dress herself. Our two-year-old with white-blonde hair and striking blue eyes wore a pair of jeans that may have belonged to an older brother at some point.

They fit, sort of, but they were not hers. Over her plain grey T-shirt was a huge medallion style necklace. If anybody could pull off this look — it was her. She was strutting down the corridor like it was a catwalk, with her bodyguards in tow. The boys were in their normal clothes and all the kids (plus Daddy too) looked tired. They were happy to see August and I, but nervous energy hung in the air.

The preacher of our church also came to visit. He prayed with us and left his card should we need anything.

I was swollen and emotional and hadn't slept, but prayerful that we'd be heading home soon. Soon. *Soon.* I kept telling myself, trying to be hopeful.

My hope was short-lived. We were waiting for petri dishes and test results and things that seemed to take far too long. By afternoon, August's fever began to creep up again. I took a picture of my family with my cell phone. I made sure to get in it, as tear stained and swollen as I was. I dare not say aloud why taking that picture was so important to me. I didn't need to say anyway, Sam already knew.

I wanted pictures and memories, no matter what. I wanted tangible proof. We were here, all of us together. I could never voice that it was "just in case". I started to prepare myself for another night without the chaos of my little family nearby. I heavily preferred chaos. We said our goodbyes again and prayed together that this would be our last night apart from one another.

I settled in for another night of sitting up, watching every breath of our littlest girl, searching the Bible, and prayer. Mixed in all of it was *The Walking Dead* marathon on television. I had seen the entire series, but it seemed to be the only thing that could distract my mind at least for a moment. HGTV wasn't cutting it anymore. I needed zombies and post-apocalyptic madness to occupy my mind a few minutes at a time.

Less than an hour after my family headed home to eat and rest, the doctor came in. His face was drawn and serious. He used a lot of words to tell me he had no idea what was wrong with our baby. He was in over his head.

"If she makes it through the night, we'll move her to the Children's Hospital an hour away."

"IF??" my heart stopped, and the question came out both loud and shaky.

"If?" I repeated more quietly, but with the same urgency.

I found reassurance in his face; not because he was reassuring, but because he so clearly *didn't know*.

"I would expect about 50/50 to see tomorrow." He shrugged his shoulders. I could tell he was trying to be compassionate but didn't know how to offer relief. He offered "I'm sorry" instead.

My face asked all the questions I had.

"Babies this age can turn so rapidly, we're doing all we can to help her, but, we just won't know more until tomorrow."
He left the room, and I turned my attention to the now twelve-pound pile of cheeks and happiness in my arms. He had to be wrong. She was just so perfect.

I called Sam to update him on the move planned for tomorrow. I couldn't bring myself to tell him any other part of the conversation. He eased my heart with the sound of his voice and calm demeanor. I wished so badly he could hug me right then.

I found great relief in knowing we could head to the Children's Hospital the next day. A new set of eyes, a new set of medical experience, an entire hospital of professionals that worked with children. Maybe they wouldn't seem as nervous as these doctors. My heart pounded for the hours to turn faster and faster. I could see a sliver of sky from the hospital room that was mostly blocked by the wall facing it. I searched for a flicker of morning until I could see the oranges and purples. The phrase, "red sky in morning, sailors take warning" rolled through my mind. I saw no red that morning. Though I'm not a sailor — I took it as a good sign.

Not too long after Sam and the kids arrived the next morning, we were ready to head out. We had all survived the night without incident. *I didn't allow myself to think back on that night and the conversation until several years after.*

Even though August had lived about 99% of her life in my arms and the other 1% in her daddy's arms, she had to ride on the stretcher for the duration of the ambulance ride.

More kisses to Sam and the kids; they'd follow the ambulance to the hospital. I would see them soon and, Lord willing, we could get some good news.

She looked so tiny in that adult sized stretcher with the straps bigger than her arms. She was perfectly content — as usual. An EMT rode in the back with us. August was on the stretcher, and I was on a small seat right next to her. I could lay my hand on her little leg. I prayed for her, for a safe ambulance ride, for more answers at the new hospital, for August's health, and for my own heart to rest.

I chatted a little with the EMT. He couldn't have been more than 22 or 23. He said he and his wife were looking for a church. I was surprised that he was married. When Sam and I married at 21, we felt like we were the only ones that married that young. Many of our friends told us we were the only ones that married that young. I was probably only ten years older than this man in charge of my daughter's life, but felt like an elder, aged by time and circumstances. He was fresh-faced and young. I told him about our church, about how we were Bible-based.

"Take nothing away from the Bible, add nothing to it." I told him, my tired mind would've been more eloquent another time. My face was swollen and tear-streaked, but I felt hopeful with what faced us on the other side of this ambulance ride.

As we spoke of God and the Bible, for the first time in nearly three days, I drifted off to sleep. My hand was still cradling the leg of my sleeping newborn as she comfortably rode within the confines of the grown-up sized stretcher. A bump in the road woke me. I apologized for falling asleep during our talk.

"No, no, ma'am. You need to rest while you can." He assured me. I recognized his maturity despite his youthful appearance. I gratefully slept the rest of the ride.

As we pulled into what seemed like an ambulance garage, they unloaded August Debra, and I followed close behind. The card my preacher left for me the day before fell from the stack of things I was carrying.

"May I keep this?" the young EMT asked after reading over it quickly.

"Of course!" I responded cheerfully, feeling like maybe I had done something for him when really, it wasn't me at all.

"Thank you so much" I told him. I could feel the tears welling in my eyes — they came so easily now. It was partly for our conversation, but mainly for the rest that my mind and heart needed so much.

There, during me only seeing what was happening in *my* moment, to *my* family, God was working on the heart of someone right in front of me and I failed to notice.

As an EMT, he is probably in the background of many people's big moments, but here he was having a moment of quiet importance right in front of me. What an honor.

Within minutes, the Children's hospital had us in a room. I could send the room number to Sam, and they'd meet me up there shortly.

Before the kids came, while it was quiet, I wanted to ask what I was scared to ask.

"My husband and kids are coming soon." I told her. The nurse was young and hurried but stopped and listened to me when I spoke. I appreciated that, having no doubt she was busy. Her face seemed worried at what I was going to ask.

"Can they stay?" I questioned, fearing we'd have the same answer as before. I was vague with my question, wanting to at least hear a possibility before the letdown.

"Oh sure!" Her response was filled with relief. I'm not sure what she thought I was asking.

Then I regretted being vague because now I had to ask more specifically. Getting my hopes up was one thing, but getting my kids' hopes up was another. I didn't want to do that.

"But I mean, like, overnight. Can they just stay here? With me and August? In the room? There are four other kids plus my husband." I overcorrected with specifics and my heart stung at not being able to say five other kids.

"Yes!" she kind of laughed. "Your whole family can stay here. Your whole family could also stay at Ronald McDonald house if you'd like more space, but they can all stay right here in the room if you want."

She continued. "We'll bring you one meal, probably for the nursing mama, and the rest of your family can bring meals in, eat at the cafeteria, or eat at the Ronald McDonald House. There's a child-life zone for playtime, and a teacher on staff to help your older kids keep up on schoolwork." She comforted and continued "You'll be fine." She patted my shoulder as she continued her work preparing the room.

"How old are your other kids?" she asked as tears of relief absolutely poured from my eyes. After I told her their ages, she went on… "We could bring a gaming system in the room for them. Do you think they'd enjoy that?"

This nurse was nothing short of an angel from Heaven to me at that moment. I wondered if she knew how grateful I was. Not only could they stay with us, but the hospital made it *easy*. It didn't matter how long we had to stay to ride this out because we could do it together. I held onto that feeling as we were alerted that it would likely be three weeks. We ordered supplies from a one-hour delivery place, including air mattresses and blankets. They moved us into a bigger room, so the boys had space to spread out a little.

Instead of the view of a hospital wall that we had previously, we had a sprawling view of the city from the 7th floor. We could see the football stadium and river. That evening, we decided the pink sky was a hello from Keely. When it started to burn red, my mind finished the rhyme "red sky at night, sailor's delight."
Despite all the scary news and scary moments, we had an abundance to be thankful for. Pretty high up on my list of gratitude was that we were already homeschooling. The boys had their regular schoolwork to do right there next to the rest of us. It passed the time and kept them up to date on their studies. We weren't home, but home was found in each other. We had a routine and a countdown.

I kept my Bible close, still Isaiah 41:10. "I will help you." And He did. Those three weeks gave us many moments close to God.

I was right in the hope I had on the move to the Children's hospital. There were no more internet searches by medical staff, at least in front of me. I was filled with gratitude that August continued to be the picture of perfection. We spent three long weeks there. We passed the time with books and movies, schoolwork and trips downstairs to play air hockey. We tried every takeout place that would deliver. We checked off the days of the calendar one by one.

I sat up at night, holding my newborn baby in the crook of my arm in the same chair I sat in throughout the day. As the sounds of my other children and husband snoring around me lowered my heart rate, I listened to the sounds in the hall. Nurses laughed and shared stories; a normal weeknight for them. I heard the occasional baby, then comfort from a nurse. I heard carts squeak down the hallway. I heard monitors beep and click. The lights of the hallway never dimmed; they beamed through the edges of the door.
We were far enough above the city lights; they didn't reach us through the window. The smell of that one certain cleaning sanitizer they used for what seemed like everything is haunting – I recognize it when I enter a hotel that uses it now. The frog picture framed

above my head was the one AD liked to stare out all the times she would wake up to look around. She probably thought this was home. I guess it was for a little while. A home I didn't want but was grateful for. A home I may not have been grateful for had it not been for those first two awful nights at a different hospital. A place that was housing my family. We brought home wherever we went.

It was sometime during those three weeks in the hospital, I posted on social media looking for a small pond someone would let me photograph my family next to. I didn't explain why.

Her fever broke as we finished up another round of IV antibiotics — it was then that the team of doctors began to solve her mystery. The day before we were ready to go home, she was diagnosed with vesicoureteral reflux. A plan was developed to keep her healthy, symptoms to watch for, and a promising long-term outlook. We met the team of urologists that would operate on her a year later.

The head surgeon looked like the doctors from the soap operas my mom watched when I was a kid. He was confident and certain in his work. His reassuring presence was exactly what we needed after spending so much time not knowing what was wrong when it seemed like nothing at all was wrong. Her doctor sat with me to explain every detail, answer every question, and make sure I understood she was going to be 100% fine and healthy. My mind was weary, and my body exhausted, so my questions became repetitive. The doctor's answers were certain— just what a tired mother needed. I recalled that conversation to counteract when fear would try to creep in over the next year.

13

Sam and I found ourselves at the pond a month after we were released from the Children's hospital. Our kids were dressed in textured neutrals, loosely coordinated, and Sam was instructed to keep hands on them at all times. I respected the water too much for it to not make me nervous. I was all the way across the pond to get the right angle.

I photographed my children in stairstep order with a spot in between Boston and Callum —where Keely should be. I photographed each one of them in her spot. We weren't far from "her" dates — *the day she died and the day she was born.* Amidst the cool air and blossoming buds, I could feel her everywhere in spring.

I wasn't sure what I was going to do with those photographs, but I was glad to have them. I printed and cherished the images I took in my studio of August as a newborn, makeup-less Mommy and all. If I learned anything, it was to take the picture. Just take the picture — so, I did. I took the pictures, uploaded them, and let them sit for a couple of months. My heart and mind needed to work together to settle on how to approach these images. It was too important to rush.

I left the folder open on my desktop. I thought about the pictures. I thought about how I could make it the tangible memory that my heart needed. I thought about how I could *show* people all my children. We had enough children now that people didn't count. When they asked how many I had, I could say six and people rarely questioned it. People rarely counted. They just saw a lot of children and assumed I knew.

Occasionally, someone would count, and I could say we have a girl that died. It gave me a chance to say her name. Though it might have made the other party uncomfortable— I could sleep at night knowing she was included.

As I caught up with studio work that piled up during our hospital stay, I found myself starting to flip through the photos. One night, with no warning from myself, it just felt like time. I sat in front of Photoshop for hours, selecting arms and legs, manipulating light, considering facial expressions. When I finally backed up and looked at the image — the tears came —and didn't stop.

There they were, all six of my children. I called Sam in, knowing he was unsure of the project. I pulled the image up as big as I could make it on my monitor. I stood far back and lowered the lights. I needed him to really see it. Tears were still flowing freely as he walked in.

He kind of chuckled with a loving comfort at my emotional state, no matter how used to it he was.

I pointed to it and waited for his reaction.

We both stared at the image before us. Five of our children on the shoreline of a pond. All six of our children in the reflection. Keely, as an eleven-year-old, was there in the reflection. She was built from the clothes and limbs and hair and faces of her siblings.

It seemed like an eternity we stood staring at this image that didn't seem possible not long before. I glanced at him and back at the photograph—then back again. His poker face gave no indication of what he thought. Normally, I appreciate his raw honesty, but I was willing him to LOVE it. These were his babies too, and he missed her as much as I missed her. Did he need to see her the way I needed to see her?

He saw me searching his face for a reaction and put his arm around my shoulder. He pulled me in close to him and I braced myself for that honesty that I so often craved.

"You did good, babe." It was the single most important critique I've received in my life. I looked up at him.

"You like it?" I was filled with excitement and wanted to share it.

"Yeah. It's wild." His face lit up with emotion in a way none of my other work ever made it. It was the exact reaction I hoped for.

When my mom came for a visit the next day, I shared it with her. I could see her start to twist herself up in a knot to spin Keely around and see her as if she were standing there. She cried with me. It was just how she pictured Keely too.

Aside from Mom, I kept the image to just Sam and I for a few more months. Not only did I not want to be weird, but I wanted to keep her private just for us for a little while. When I decided it was time to share the image, I uploaded it to my photography business social media page.

I wanted it to be public, but I also wanted my friends and family to see it. I wanted the support of the mamas who had been where I was. It didn't get old, seeing those beautiful faces all lined up next to each other. It was met with a huge reception of love and likes. Many people asked how they could get one.

I began to think about how I could get them one and began to plan for an exhibition of images just like this one —each one unique and telling the story of the children in it.

The theme and location could be determined by the family's interests. The more I thought about it, the more intricate and layered the storytelling became.

In this season of life, we were traveling extensively as a family. To the south for a long weekend one month, then the east coast the next. Each month brought us to a new corner of the country. The gaming tournaments for our kids forced us to put these dates and places in our schedule when planning a vacation would've been put off to a more convenient time. It was perfect. Our kids were enjoying success at something they loved and even Sam played in some tournaments. I was grateful, once again, to be homeschooling the kids so we could travel.

Our first major tournament was in San Francisco, so we made it into the all-American road trip. We took a faster route through northern states on the way there, searching the foothills for wild horses and bears. We stopped at historic sites, and I read aloud on the way to them, so we'd know what we were looking at. We detoured often to find cute local vegan restaurants and, if we were lucky, desserts too. After several days on the California coast reveling at how many enormous bowls of noodles Marnie could ingest, we meandered our way back through the central states to Indiana. We weren't even back home yet when they announced the next year's grand finale tournament would be in Anaheim, California. So, we planned the great American road trip, take two.

Most often, we had just a few moments to meet up with each family. We passed through some cities or detoured off our path to meet families at sports parks and in hotel gyms. We met in parking lots and fields on the side of the road. I used a green screen and often brought lights when space allowed. I called ahead to find specific locations and ask permission. Many emails and calls from businesses didn't get returned, but the people that did respond were filled with compassion for the families and excitement for the project. Anticipation built as each concept was tailored to each family.

The families filled out questionnaires, asking what their child looked like, how old he or she would be, and if they had a special stuffed animal or lovey. You know, the basics.

I also asked harder questions. What do you believe your child would look like *now*? What personality traits do you imagine your child having? Then the hardest question: What do you want people to know about your story? That one set everybody back.

With each scheduled bereavement session, I met a family who had walked a path similar to ours. With many of those meetings, I got to hug the mother who carried me when the weight was too much to bear alone. I was able to look into the eyes of the mother whose stories I knew so well. I cried and prayed for them after each session. I felt a tremendous pressure to present to them the perfect commemoration of their child's life.

We spent a cold evening on a dark Memphis street photographing one family. I had known the mother since I had worked up the courage to post on the online board for grieving mothers. She was one of the first women to comfort me. We had cried and remembered together so many times over the past 10+ years. We offered comfort on hard dates and harder days. We said their names out loud. Before meeting that December, I spoke to an optometrist that had their front window decorated for Christmas. He was so proud of the work his staff had put into their display and was happy to share that for my work. When I told him what project I was working on, he choked up.

"Happy to help."

I wondered what part of his story the pathway to his compassion was. The sun went down quicker than I had expected, but the street was lit up with holiday lights and low streetlamps. No pink in the sky that night – it was too cloudy. The snowmen in the windows twinkled. As the flash triggered to the side of my camera, the sides of my friend's living children lit up. In that instant, it was as if I could see the face of the little girl I had to create through her sibling's reflections. In those images, the final image kind of formed itself. We said our goodbyes after a brief visit, and my family and I walked back to our hotel. Just as the hotel was in sight, a few snowflakes twirled around us. Another little hello.

I wasn't checking the names off the list as fast as I wanted to, but I was chiseling away at a mountain. When we got home from each trip, I would back up the images in as many places as I could come up with and then set them aside. It was a mountain I had to climb, but I couldn't do it all at once. My heart wouldn't allow that.

Life was the easiest it had ever been. I soaked in having my children home with me like it was the way we were meant to live. A routine that was pretty set, but I adjusted slightly as their curriculum changed and the weather called for us to be outside.

Family walks and neighborhood scavenger hunts occupied warm days. August's inaugural trip to Disney World with my parents kicked off a new year right around her first birthday. We also went to Disneyland that summer for a gaming tournament. Each Disney trip, we collected a pin in Keely's memory and brought it home to a pink lanyard that adorned her sisters' wall.

In the meantime, my studio work picked up enough that we were there most days at some point or another. On weekends we weren't traveling I was in the studio, and my mom came to assist when we needed help. The reason we lived where we lived was to have my parents in our children's lives as regularly as we could. I had been so spoiled having my grandma Marney and Gramps within arm's reach. There's a certain level of comfort a child (or adult for that matter) can't reach without constant contact.

I always searched for light days for a visit from my mom too, my kids' "Nana". Those days were my favorite. We could sit by the pool and let the kids splash for hours. Mom could hold a sleeping baby. We could all enjoy donuts. My mom lived to see her grandchildren joyful – she made it her mission. Our schedule was full and so were our hearts —all missions accomplished.

We were on our way home from one of our trips, and our route took us straight through my parents' town. Everybody was tired, so we decided to stop at Mom and Dad's house "just for a few minutes" to let the kids give their grandparents hugs, talk about the weekend, and use the bathroom for the final stretch home.

As soon as we walked in, we all took that deep breath that being in a comfortable place offers. The few minutes turned into a few hours very quickly, as we all knew they would. My oldest sister's children were at Mom and Dad's too while their parents finished up Christmas shopping. The cousins got to play together and occupy one another so Mom and I could visit.

She was tired, but in good spirits as she tended to be for the holiday season. She had been so exhausted that fall and just kept going. I found myself frustrated with her pace at times.

"Mom, if you'd just rest for a few days and put an old black and white movie on to relax, you'd feel better." I continued as if our roles were reversed. "You'll never get rid of that cough if you don't REST." I emphasized the same words to her that she would to me.

"Honey, I'll rest when I'm all caught up." She assured me, knowing full well she'd never really be caught up.

The sun was long gone by the time we said our goodbyes late into that evening. Mom handed out "Nanny candy" in individual Ziploc bags and a separate one of Skittles to each of the kids. Since August barely had teeth and was still nursing, she got a Ziploc bag of puffs —basically baby cheesy puffs. My sister's kids were still there when we left, so the receiving line of hugs and goodbyes was long.

With less than a week until Christmas — the excitement was building. My parents had twelve grandchildren in just over twelve years. Each of those kids would end up with the exact same amount of money spent and the exact same number of presents. The matter of equality for her grandchildren was the top of her list.

The next morning, I talked to my mom on the phone as I did each day after Sam left for work. We talked about the food for Christmas, *check*. Which wrapping paper for which grandkid, *check*. The times to expect us for Christmas, and the separate times to expect my sisters' families which differed from the times they'd actually arrive, *check*. We talked about holiday movies and reminisced on a frantic search through a shopping mall in 1991.

My mom was desperately looking for an old black and white movie for her favorite cousin. "Christmas in Connecticut" was nowhere to be found in the two stores we had in town. Mom made phone calls all over. Eventually, she found it at a store an hour away, and we celebrated. My mother took great care to consider what gift receivers would truly enjoy. I still think of my mom's favorite cousin every time I watch that movie.

The week continued to be filled with excitement the way the week before Christmas tends to be with many little children to invoke the holiday spirit. We probably watched Charlie Brown Christmas three dozen times. Mornings brought my daily phone call with mom. Sometimes, especially on busy days, it would be cut shorter than normal. On a relaxed day with not much on the schedule, we could stretch it into two or three hours. The kids would jump on the calls or finish up their reading and other tasks.

This week, we both had a lot going on. Thursday was mom's wrapping day. She had, quite literally, hundreds of gifts to wrap. She had diagrams and lists as if she were planning to go to war. She was a woman on a mission. This kept our Thursday call short.

She reported the next morning that she wrapped presents for twelve straight hours. She was frustrated with herself for not finishing. All that was left were the gifts for my sisters and me. She calculated that she probably had an hour or so to finish.

"I should've just done it." She told mostly herself, but me too.

"Mom" in my adult bratty voice, "I told you we could come help you wrap those!" I meant it. I thought it would be fun for my sisters and I to wrap the presents, drink coffee, and be festive, just the grownups. I figured we'd have it done in a few hours. But I also knew of Mom's lists and diagrams and doublechecking. She trusted us, just not enough to handle her grandkids' Christmas presents.

Later that evening, I got a call from my dad. That's unusual, I thought to myself as his name popped up on my cell phone.

"Hey Chooch." Dad said, using his nickname for me.

"Hey Dad" I answered. Before I could even ask about sports or the weather or some other mundane thing, he continued. "We're going to have to push Christmas back. Mom's just having a hard time shaking this bug."

"Aw man, I'm sorry. Poor Mom!" We had to push holidays around before for illnesses of varying degrees. We'd just move it back a week to New Years. It didn't seem like that big of a deal to me, but the tone in my father's voice did. He seemed nervous — even distracted.

We had December 25th at home, just our little family. It was a special day, but different. I flooded my mom's cell phone with pictures of the day. I knew she'd be sad to not be seeing the kids, so I wanted her to feel like she was there. A picture of them on the stairs in their red pajamas. We had the same one from my parents' house every other year and my grandparents' home before that. I thought she could just hear their squeals from the blurry images of sheer delight when they opened their presents. And of course, the pictures of the aftermath — a mountain of torn wrapping paper and boxes that seemed much larger than a few hours before. I knew she wouldn't want to miss a thing.

I pictured my parents at home in the living room I grew up in, with their picture-perfect Christmas tree, listening to Bing Crosby records in their red pajamas. We called to say hi a few times that day but kept the conversations short. Chaos on my end of the call and more rest needed on Mom's end.

Our morning conversations continued but cut off earlier than normal so Mom could get much needed rest. I was relieved she was taking time for herself as I had been encouraging her to do. Each day, she felt marginally better than the day before.

One morning, a few days past Christmas, our conversation turned to the reality tv show we were watching at the time. We shared the guilty pleasure of trashy tv that probably didn't contain much reality. We were catching up on the antics of semi-celebrities when Mom dropped in that she wasn't going to be up to have Christmas on New Years either.

I stopped myself from asking any more questions because I didn't want her to get anxious. We'd have Christmas whenever she was rested. It would prolong the celebrations anyway and we hadn't recovered from our sugar highs, I reassured myself. Despite my attempt to convince myself everything was fine — the pit that had formed in my stomach told me otherwise.

14

"Well, I think I'm at the end of my life."

The words hung in the air and the room started to spin on my end of the phone. Before I could respond, she continued. "I've had a good life. Everyone gets to this point."

"I've had a good life." She repeated herself, this time with more vigor.

"Mom." I wasn't quite sure what to say. I felt certain she was overreacting. She was rundown and tired from doing too much.

"Mom, what are you talking about?" I repeated the same sentiment I had several times over the last month or so. "You haven't taken a day to yourself. Just REST." I emphasized again, feeling my heart pound in my ears.

"You have the same bug that the kids have had." I tried to ease her fear by reminding her that my kids and my sister's kids had bad colds that week — *normal winter stuff.*

"This is different, Alyson." Alyson. She never called me by my full name unless it was serious, and I knew I wasn't in trouble right now. Not from her anyway.

"Mom, why don't you go see a doctor. Maybe you just need an antibiotic or a lung x-ray or something." I wanted to encourage her. My mother did not like to go to the doctor. She had too much history of doctors failing her. Thankfully, she hadn't needed to be seen by a medical professional for several years.

She accompanied us to many appointments, got the flu shot while August was in the hospital, and did what she could — but away from the doctor's office.

I expected the usual pushback from her when I suggested a visit to the doctor. Instead, I sense something I didn't expect in her voice — *fear.*

"I just don't want to go in anywhere." She pleaded.

"What if they could come to you? Would that make you feel better?" I still felt certain she was just…nervous. As we spoke, I was googling home healthcare, nurses, and anything else I could think of that would help ease her mind. My little hometown didn't offer many options.

Then I thought of the man I had a locker next to in Junior High. My maiden last name started with C. His last name started with D. He was a doctor now in my parents' town. *Maybe he'd have a lead for me.* I sent him a message on social media. Before my mom and I had even gotten off the phone, he responded that he would stop by.

This wasn't something that he normally did, but he took pity on his locker neighbor from twenty years before. I said a prayer of gratitude to God for the way things worked in the small town I grew up in.

I verified with my mom that she was okay with it, and much to my surprise —she was. I gave my dad's phone number to the guy I hadn't seen since high school graduation, but I knew we had stood next to each other then. He would be at their house in less than an hour.

In a rush to get off the phone, my mom said, "I guess I'd better tell you everything then."

I thought she already did. I braced myself as she explained to me that she found a lump on her spine a few weeks before. She had only mentioned it to my dad. Nobody ever said the word "cancer" in front of my mom; she had heard that word too many times in her family already. She certainly didn't say it. It wasn't said this day either, but it was implied.

A flurry of texts from my dad within minutes alerted me that my locker-neighbor-turned-doctor believed the lumps were cancer.

Lumps. Plural.

Mom and Dad headed to the doctor's office to get more testing done. Turns out, the doctor just seeing her at her home wouldn't be enough and now she was being forced into the doctor's office. *The very place she didn't want to be.*

My heart sank. I *knew* it wasn't cancer, but my mother was having another medical scare. I was trying to help her, and here she was heading into a doctor's office, her own personal hell. She was everywhere she didn't want to be because I interfered.

My hands shook. I prayed. I waited. I texted Sam at work, afraid to say anything that the kids might hear. Afraid to say it aloud at all. Afraid to speak cancer into existence.

My parents had been at the doctor's office for hours when we finally heard from them. It was late in the day and all we found out was we had more waiting to do. *Why do these things always happen on Fridays?*

For the first time in my life, I was scared to talk to my mom. I felt terrible for being the catalyst to a weekend of anxious waiting when I was just trying to help. I was embarrassed at my mistake.

Now, because of me, she was going to spend an entire weekend steeped in anxiety that she had *it*. I knew she didn't. I *knew* it. I still wouldn't say the word.

How foolish to think the kid with the locker next to me all those years before was doing something helpful. How quickly I had jumped to conclusions, thinking I knew a way to help.

My dad and I never talked on the phone, and when we did, it was short and informative.

This was different, the guilt was eating me alive, so I called my dad. "Does Mom hate me?" I asked, both loving and hating that Dad wouldn't dance around any facts.

"For what?" he asked as if there may be multiple reasons.

"For calling the doctor. For all the worrying." I braced myself.

"Oh no, Chooch." He sounded surprised as if the thought hadn't crossed his, or her, mind. Needing additional confirmation, I summoned the courage to call Mom and find out for myself.

"Hi, Honey." she answered quickly, without giving me the opportunity to overthink.

"Hi Mom, how are you feeling?" Waiting with bated breath to hear her tone towards me.

She was giving me all the same answers she had been the week before, but I could hear the uncertainty in her voice.

"Are you mad at me?" I barely let her finish answering my previous question because I had to ask.

"No babe. I knew this was coming. You were helping." She knew why I thought she'd be mad. Now I knew she wasn't, but I think I would have preferred her anger to her fear. It echoed through the phone.

"You're good, mom." I reassured her. "You'll be relieved a week from now." I was so certain.

Despite her not being mad, I felt so terrible for involving her in doctor's appointments and a weekend of worry. We sent flowers and I went to see her the next day and help pass the time waiting for the weekend to end.

Monday morning couldn't come fast enough and, when it did, brought the good news that we were hoping to hear. It wasn't even 8 AM when I got the text from my dad that Mom's tests were all good. Her kidneys and liver were clear. They wanted her to come in for more tests and to rehydrate. Okay, sounds like a relief to me.

If they were to find cancer now, at least it wouldn't be widespread. *Beatable*. Okay, that's all I needed to hear, to tell myself, to calm down.

For as certain as I was to my mom and when I spoke, a big part of me was terrified. When I'm faced with dramatic and sometimes traumatic situations, I tend to take the opposite sentiment of those around me. If everyone is optimistic and sure of a good outcome, I feel like I'm jinxing it. If everyone is certain of bad news — I take on the role of Pollyanna — all sunshine and roses.

Though I hadn't planned on being able to come visit mom, Sam took the day off work so I could show up impulsively. I wanted to be there to celebrate and breathe. I needed to see my mother's relief with my own eyes. I texted my sisters on the way, and it was a surprise to my mom. She was happy to see me and eventually all three of her daughters were there, along with Dad, in her hospital room with her.

It had been many years since it was just the five of us, no husbands or grandchildren. I felt like a kid again, but in the worst way. I had been hoping to find an air of relief, but it was filled with, at best, reservation.

My Mom knew more information was coming — it was written all over her face. Even though I had the same information everyone else had, I felt uninformed and ignorant as to what was coming. *And I was.*

Sam was able to work his schedule so I could go back the next day too. I was getting spoiled, but knew I needed to be there. Tuesday was filled with learning how Mom could handle her newly diagnosed diabetes and more tests — so many tests.

My sisters and I had lunch in the cafeteria to give Mom and Dad time alone. A lone, seemingly old banana was the only option for me in the small-town cafeteria of the hospital. My stomach was filled with anxiety, my appetite nowhere to be found. When I needed to leave to get back to the kids, we had no new news at that point. However, shortly after I got home that evening, —the phone rang.

It was my oldest sister. Her voice was unsteady. She whispered in a low tone. "Aly, it's cancer. It's bad." She explained the doctor came in shortly after the sun set and I hit the road for home. There was cancer in her lungs, cancer in her kidneys, cancer in her lymph nodes. We would know more in the coming days, but the doctor believed it to have come from her kidney. Our phone call was brief, and we ended with an agreement that there would be more waiting. *There seemed to always be more waiting and less information than we craved.*

That evening, I searched all the corners of the internet for information to ease my fears. I found every hopeful story I could, but I found many, many more without the happy ending I sought out. I scoured cancer boards for her specific type and searched recent posts to see if they were still alive. I spent the night praying in between all the information I could find. I searched the risk factors. *She fit into exactly zero of them. Zero risk factors for kidney cancer. Zero risk factors for lung cancer. Zero. I couldn't find any logic in that diagnosis.*

As much as I don't want to admit it now, I wasn't ready to give it away to God. Not yet. I would just cure cancer. I went to God for that. *Guide me, Lord. Help me find answers.* The only solution I found acceptable was a complete and total cure, or better yet, a medical mistake and she was actually fine.

I'd have to wait for them to discover their mistake while I combed through everything from the medical journals and studies to companies preying on cancer patients, promising a cure. In all my research, I kept returning to her risk factors or lack thereof. *Were they wrong or was this the lightning strike that's always possible in medical situations?* None of this made any sense.

The first days after her official diagnosis passed in a rotating cloud of fatigue, hope, and despair. We heard many different opinions, including doctors that gave worst case scenario with no hope and even less bedside manner. We heard from nurses who had survived kidney cancer and said if they had to pick a cancer to get, this would be it. *The cancer jackpot.* It didn't feel like it.

The information received seemed to change daily, along with the plan and prognosis. The only thing that never changed was the waiting. We always had more waiting to do.

In a few days, Mom's strength improved, and she was moved to the fourth floor, the rehabilitation floor. She'd be back at Orchard Hill soon, where she could get well. Orchard hill was her comfort, and her sanctuary. Surely, she could improve better in the home that gave her so much life.

She grew up on the same property, half a mile away. She played as a child on the hill my parents built their home. She wrote poems about her trips "up the hill" with her cousins and built her home on that same soil years later. My mother raised her three daughters among the apple trees that were planted on the Hoosier hills long before our family came to be. She would thrive at home — right where she was meant to be. She would thrive at home just as she always had.

It wasn't the first time Orchard Hill would soften the impact of sickness and death.

***

Ten days after Thanksgiving 1990, it was my 9th birthday. My mom always made a big deal out of birthdays. She'd take me to Arnold's Bakery the week before so I could pick out a pan shape for my cake. It was in a rough part of town, but the smell was enough to risk it. The smell of butter and sugar —the absolute magic of childhood. I picked Snoopy out that year. They'd dot little stars of icing all over it and it would harden before we'd get it home. The tablecloth on our dining room table was red with silver holiday trim- the fanciest. Balls of sherbert bobbed around and fizzed in a crystal bowl filled with 7 Up. Mom would use the real silver and I'd get to wear the crown she'd won as prom queen in 1969.

I spent my birthdays being treated like a queen. My dad's parents always made the trek from about an hour and a half away, not getting home until close to midnight. Grandpa always forgot his hat. He'd leave it sitting on the bench by the entryway. I don't know if these things happened once, or if they really happened continually. A memory forever etched in my mind.

I didn't appreciate as a child how big of a trip it was for them to make that drive every year, but I do now. That year, for my 9th birthday, they gave me a flowery denim skirt and a new baby doll. My greatest dilemma that night was which new skirt to wear to school the next day with black leggings underneath.

Just as the party was getting underway — the phone rang. Mom talked in a whispered tone, tethered to the wall, back in the day before the convenience of cordless phones. She twirled the yellow phone cord that had been stretched out by my teenage sisters. Her face was drawn when she turned around. She and my dad stepped into the breezeway to greet my mom's sister, who lived down the hill with my grandparents. The three of them came back in without making eye contact. The party went on.

I opened my presents, joked with my sisters about boys and New Kids on the Block. I ate cake and went to bed much later than usual. I noticed my grandparents weren't there. I assumed when my mom said my grandma Marney didn't feel well that year, she had a little bug and we'd see her soon. I knew she would "make up" for missing my party and we'd have an extra party of our own. I was looking forward to keeping the celebration going. A few days later, after a big hug and reunion, we had a normal Sunday dinner at Pleasant Ridge, cooked by my grandmother.

After dinner, the women chatted in the kitchen doing dishes, and my Gramps snored in a recliner with a football game on the tv. I was choreographing dances to Milli Vanilli, and the sunlight seemed the same to me. Everything was back to normal.

Sort of.

Normal now was my grandma Marney in and out of the hospital. Normal now was playing board games with her over playing in the yard. Boggle and Go Fish were perfect – I didn't mind a bit. Normal now was a hospital bed in the living room. She'd let me curl up on it next to her and watch Bette Midler movies.

Most of those movies went over my head, but it didn't matter. I'd eat slices of American cheese with smarties candies pressed into them. She wouldn't even gag at that. I'd draw pictures to bring her. The last one I drew hung on the fridge for somewhere around 20 years. We never changed it after that spring.

As a kid, nobody really knows how to help you through grief. Adults to kids in grief are like throwing a life vest to someone just swimming. The swimmer doesn't need help, but the lifeguards think they couldn't possibly be doing it on their own.

Kids are probably actually better at it than adults, but we can't let them know that. They'd be too powerful. They just keep living. They keep living the way the adults try to do, but are clouded by thoughts and worries, what ifs and maybes. Kids *live*.

Instead, us adults just end up kind of watching the bereaved children and encourage them and offer them candy and more television shows than normal. *Then we try to guide because that's what adults are supposed to do, right?*

I'll let you in on a secret – even the most grown up of adults don't feel like they know what they're doing. Often in grief, everything feels wrong. As adjusting to my grandma's health condition became a new normal, I can recall a special time with her that I wouldn't trade for anything.

I went through an awkward time during 3rd grade where I was always at the dentist. My head was growing into my giant teeth, but not without gum pains and a few cavities. I didn't even mind it, because it was a chance to get out of school when the light was still high in the sky. It felt so weird to be out of school during a weekday in winter. Why is that? Why did it all look so different? I felt like a spy on a covert mission. *Would people wonder if I were a celebrity? Why else would this child be roaming the streets during a weekday afternoon? Was she a child genius and getting ready to join Doogie Houser to perform surgery?*

I imagined all the amazing things people would think about me, but I was beyond thrilled when my dad treated me to lunch at Wendy's after my dentist appointment. I basically *was* a celebrity at that point.

I enjoyed my spicy chicken sandwich and fries slowly. I liked this time with my dad. I had a chocolate frosty to mark this special occasion.

With a mouth full of chicken, I blurted out "I want to go to the hospital to see my Grandma Marney."

My mom would've reminded me to swallow my food before talking, but my dad gave me a side eye.

After a pause, he said "Are you just trying to run out the school clock?"

"Nope" I said quickly. I knew he'd think that and was ready to show him I meant business. He never actually answered me, but turned left out of the Wendy's parking lot after I finished my sandwich.

The hospital smelled of cold steel and cleaning supplies. Sometimes a musty aroma might creep in, but that was fleeting. I had only been inside it a few times before. It was a little county hospital that had been a house a hundred years prior, but enough additions made it seem huge now.

My Gramps was a candy-striper there and I'd go with him occasionally. He said I was a good distraction and a good visitor. He even taught me some magic tricks to show the patients. Much to my disappointment, I never got a uniform to wear.

I didn't remember this smell from the times I'd been there before. It seemed…scary.

I walked down the long hall with my dad and grabbed his hand. At the mature age of 9, it wasn't often that I held my dad's hand anymore. As the youngest of the family, it was always my mission to demonstrate how grown-up I was. I needed his hand now, though.

We went up one flight of stairs and I saw some of my aunts by a door farther down the hallway. None of them were actual aunts, but that's what I called them anyway.

I suddenly second-guessed myself. There were a lot of people there. I knew them all, but they all seemed different here. I was scared. But I was also scared to admit I'd been wrong to come. School wasn't looking so bad right now.

They saw us coming down the hallway and one went into the room without acknowledging we were there. I was sure I'd made a mistake.

Just as my eyes darted around for an escape route, my Gramps came out of the room he'd been in. He tucked a handkerchief into his front pocket to give me a big, tight bear hug.

"I have something to show you, Sug." he said, grabbing my hand and calling me by part of my nickname "Sugarlump". His southern accent almost always prevented him from pronouncing the p at the end.

My dad stayed back in the crowded room, where my aunts seemed like security detail for my grandmother. Gramps and I took the "back way" through the hospital, which could only be taken by the elite (or so I told myself). Everybody there knew my Gramps. He had a nickname for each of them too.

We ended up in the little gift shop by the front doors. The afternoon sun was beaming in that day- that elusive school daylight. I was glad to be near the windows again. The brightness made everything seem less scary. The room was small. A grown adult could probably reach all 4 corners from one spot. We looked at the balloons and cards. The balloon had deflated, and I wondered how long it had been there. My Gramps bought me a little necklace that looked like a class ring for a baby. It had my birthstone in it – blue topaz. It sparkled in the afternoon light. He also picked out a bunny necklace. It was a sparkly bunny pendant on a light blue ribbon with little beads on either side. You had to tie it just right or the bunny would flip over. It was perfect for spring as Easter was coming up.

I felt a little embarrassed by the gifts as I hadn't come to get something, though it wasn't a surprise from my Gramps. I worried what my dad might think. When we got back to the room where grown cousins mingled, my dad didn't seem to notice.

I walked into the room with my grandma Marney in the bed and she clapped her hands together when she saw me.

"Sugarlump!" She seemed… fine.

My nerves eased up with a hug from my seemingly fine grandmother. I felt my mom's hand tap my shoulder and reach around for a hug. She hadn't expected to see me. I was supposed to be at the dentist and then go right back to school. She also didn't know I had been to Wendy's — Dad was busted.

My mom's eyes were red. Everybody in the room had red eyes, but I avoided eye contact with the other adults. The mood seemed light. Maybe they needed the time I spent with Gramps in the gift shop to lighten it. I appreciated that. I sat on the bed with my grandmother and showed her the treasures Gramps had gotten for me. I took them out of the small paper bag that my hands had been sweating all over and purposely avoided my parents while discussing my spring jewelry.

After my impromptu visit, we were back at school with merely enough time to grab my bookbag and homework, just after the special light had faded out.

We went back to the hospital a week or so later for Easter Sunday. This time, she wasn't fine. She was sick, visibly sick. She didn't make much eye contact. She didn't move around, but she handed me a little bunny rabbit in a box.

The bunny felt velvety and had a little yellow dress on. She patted my hand in both of hers. I'll never forget how her skin felt — dry and strong —same as always. They shook a bit. Her energy was just

—gone. By morning, so was she. Death came for her before she could return to Pleasant Ridge one more time.

15

As much as we prayed, it wasn't time for Mom to go home from the hospital yet. We received information little by little to the point we had to say the words aloud. We told people so they could pray for her, pray for the doctors, and pray for us. *Pray, pray, pray.*

Mom was working hard to improve. I could see her struggling to appear better when she just wanted to rest. She had known, in fact, that she'd face cancer for thirty years. She didn't know because of risk factors or medical tests, but because she prepared to face the same battle most of the women in our family had faced. She knew it was only a matter of time, and it was her battle now.

Our schedules adjusted, our sleep disintegrated, and our prayers got louder. My Dad, sisters, and I divided up who we needed to call. We bickered lightly over the easier calls to make, the easier people to talk to, and the harder calls to make — the people who would say the wrong thing.

I either got lucky or was persistent enough to get two of my favorite people to call. *Being the baby of the family still comes in handy in your thirties occasionally.* One was Mom's first cousin. They'd been raised like sisters. My mother's cousin was five years her senior and Mom looked up to her carefree spirit. Her cousin had seen some hard times in her life, but it never dampened her joyful spirit. She was easy to talk to, fun, and honest.

When she and Mom got together, they laughed like teenagers. During many family reunions, she and mom, along with other cousins, sisters, and aunts would congregate in the small kitchen of Pleasant Ridge at the end of the day. They'd handwash dishes, tell stories, and occasionally break out in song. They'd drink sweet tea with ice clanking around on the glass. The little folded up napkins their glasses sat on would stick to them as they were raised to their mouths.

The kitchen in my grandparents' house was a quick walk through the woods from my own house, but a link to the generations that had come and gone. They lived in the stories and songs that rose through the night in the women who told them and sang. Peeking in on those evenings or sitting on various laps during those moments, I was a spectator of something I expected to continue indefinitely. Though the people might come and go, I assumed the times in the kitchen would continue. *I was wrong.*

I pictured my mom and her cousin and their lighthearted visits when I went to make that phone call. Though she was easy to talk to, this wasn't an easy call to make. I was grateful to be talking to her, though.

"Aly?" She answered, as if she had been ready to hear the news. I didn't know how she knew but was relieved I didn't have to start from the beginning. I filled her in on the important details and followed up with the rest. *For all the information we had gotten, it didn't feel like we really knew much at all.*

Towards the end of our chat, she said as her voice cracked, "Your mom is tough. She is tough." She paused momentarily, but I knew she wasn't finished. *"Tough."* She emphasized it more each time she said the word — willing her strength to my mother.

"You tell her she's going to be just fine because she must be. She comes from a long line of stubborn old women. She must be stubborn now. You tell her to call me." She continued, "Please let me know any updates, Aly. Any of them, good or..." She trailed off and there was a longer than necessary pause.

"She can call me whenever she wants to, in the middle of the night or early in the morning. She can always call me." It wasn't her words that were moving to me, but the emotion spilling from them. My eyes flooded, but I kept my tears from falling with my own stubbornness from that same line of old women.

I considered how my mom and her cousin had been where my sisters and I were right now. They faced cancer in the generation ahead of them long before they were ready, when they felt like children still.

They had always seemed grown up to me, but they hadn't always been grown up. The wisdom and maturity I knew them as having had come from hard diagnoses and harder goodbyes. I realized then how long it had been since anyone gathered in my grandparents' kitchen.

The day after, Mom was sitting up in her bed eating some cantaloupe and cottage cheese. The room seemed brighter and cheerier than it had before. Mom was eating something that I remembered her eating for breakfast when I was a kid on summer break from school. Cottage cheese still seemed gross to me, but Mom was eating, which was a glorious sight. For any of the ever-changing treatment plans to start, she had to gain some strength. This was a start. I felt optimistic. She finished eating much sooner than I had hoped. I mean she stopped eating. *I guess baby steps would have to be enough.*

I was excited to share with her the phone conversations I had the day before. She needed to know so many people were praying for her. I knew she wouldn't want the attention, but it was a relief to have the beginning of some answers. As I told her about the call with her first cousin, I saw tears form in her eyes. It was the first time I saw her cry since she got sick. It would be the only time.

"She just makes me think of being a kid." Mom explained to me, unsuccessfully choking back more tears. Her voice shook. I didn't see my mother cry very often. My sisters and I used to tease her, calling her stone-cold Debbie, as we explained to our children that she was a very different Nana than the mother who had raised us and stayed vigilant to keep us out of trouble.

I sat on the edge of the hospital bed and patted her hand the way she had done for me so many times in my life.

"It's good to cry sometimes, Mom." I reasoned. She needed the release.

We struggled with Sam's job allowing him to be home with the kids so I could be there with Mom. No amount of time spent with mom eased the guilt I felt for being unable to be there all the time. No amount of time at home with my kids eased the guilt of being unable to be with them all the time.

We adjusted our plans for a schedule we could maintain long-term. I prepared for a schedule change that would last years. My photography studio clients were like angels to me – every one of them willing to adjust their session times and extend grace. I wasn't the same person they were used to.

I was tired and anxious with dark shadows under my eyes. No matter how tired I felt, I kept working for my financial and emotional health. I kept homeschooling my kids, though the real lessons they were learning were outside of books. They learned lessons that I wasn't ready to teach them —ones I didn't want them to have to learn. We felt so far from the time we could take deep breaths, feeling settled, un-anxious for what the next day might bring. We took each day minute-by-minute now.

Anytime I had a new baby, Mom would come to my sessions with me and care for my little one. She was the only one I ever trusted with my kids. I sat with one client at the end of her baby's session. I was exhausted but trying not to show it. She asked how I was doing. I gave a shrug. I didn't have words. I was probably too honest with my clients about the situation with my mom, but it was hard not to be since many of them knew her personally.

"I have friends whose mothers died, and they were just never the same." She said to me as she patted my hand.

I stared at her for what seemed like hours. *Whose mother is dying? How dare she?*

"Oh, well. We aren't there." I paused and prepared for more tears. "She's not. She's not dying." I responded fully sure of myself.

"Right. Of course." She left soon after. I stayed a little while longer, gathering my camera and the strength to drive home.

There were some days I came to appreciate the hour-long drive between my hometown and where my family lived at the time. It allowed me time to listen to the emotional minefield of music and find tears in every lyric. Macklemore's lyrics about the good old days and Canyon's City heart that slows down took the wheel for me many days, almost always before the sun rose or after it set – never during daylight hours.

It allowed me time to turn the music off altogether and pray aloud. It allowed me conversations with God, filled with fear and anxiety, hope and guidance. I worked out a lot of feelings on the road between my hometown and my home — the same way I had between Pleasant Ridge and Orchard Hill as a child.

Other days, especially days Sam had to work, he and the kids would ride along with me. If he had to go into the office that day, we'd pick him up and drive out of town immediately. Since Mom didn't want the kids to see her sick, Sam would take the kids to wander around Walmart for three hours.

They'd spend money on junk food and silly games. It was the only place in town to waste that kind of time. If she was in the hospital, they'd spend time at my parents' house watching television. When it was time for them to pick me up to go home, Sam would encourage me to sleep while I could. Most of the time though, my mind kept me awake.

We had family meetings with the doctors. They would meet whichever sister was there with Mom for the day. Each one had slightly different information than the other, therefore, our perspectives were different. When the main oncologist called a meeting with all of us, we were hopeful for some clarity and maybe even…hope.

I came armed with a notebook full of questions, a blank one to take notes, and a pen. I was expecting a medical degree from Google any day now for all my time spent researching.

I talked myself into liking this doctor. He was our only option because Mom wanted to be close to home. He only came to town once every two weeks, sometimes once a week. *Which seemed like… not enough.*

I missed the doctor I had that didn't sugarcoat anything. I had always liked that I felt like she was laying it all on the table. I didn't get that feeling now. Though he was being honest, he was being delicate too. I didn't like that. I wanted to feel like my questions were answered completely. I missed the confidence of August's surgeon at the Children's Hospital. These doctors were anything but confident.

Our meeting was lengthy and comprehensive. He explained the different pathways her treatment plan could take. We talked about best case scenarios and lightly dusted over the opposite. He agreed to some alternative options to try in conjunction with chemo and radiation.

I had found a Canadian supplement that had miracle testimonies, seemingly hundreds of them. I became a person I wouldn't have recognized before — I bought into it. *What if. What if.* My usual skepticism was replaced by what if. *What if that's the answer. What if that's the answer and I ignore it.*

I couldn't take that chance. I put a rush order in from Canada and prayed that would be the difference maker. I prayed anything would. I let myself believe that this modern-day snake oil might just be what they said it was because I knew we needed a miracle. *I just didn't let myself say it out loud.*

The doctor let us know that her eating *anything* was better than focusing on diabetic friendly foods. I could stop working on perfecting the recipe for diabetic friendly brownies that were disgusting anyway.

Any energy she could take in was necessary now. He talked about risks and options but hadn't mentioned any cold hard numbers. I wasn't about to ask – I learned that from professor google.

Mom hadn't read that, though. This woman, who had been laying down for about a month now between home and then the hospital, perked up for that conversation and blurted out, "What are my chances to survive this?"

I don't know that I gasped audibly, but my entire body clenched up and blood ran cold. The pulse in the room stopped completely. I had seen the odds. Every which way I searched, looking for a hopeful answer gave me everything but that. One word was messing up every search and skewing every result.

Sarcomatoid.

That single word was the one that changed the odds sizably with every search. I adjusted the phrasing every which way I could, but this one word ruined it every time.

8%.

Single digit chance of survival five years from diagnosis. I reasoned with my search results that we had been on the losing side of less than 1% before, so maybe we were due to be on the winning side of 8%.

All of this ran through my head the instant my mother asked this seemingly knowledgeable, but maybe not completely forthright doctor his opinion for her odds of survival. *Survival.* Her odds of just being alive five years from now or even one year from now. *Suddenly, I found myself secretly praying he would continue to be delicate with his words.*

I could see the hesitation on his face. *Did she?* I glanced at her, back at him, and then at my dad who watched it all with bated breath.

"If I had to put a number on it", he started. I found relief in his leading statement. "I would say 30, maybe even 40 percent."

Oh. Okay, that number was significantly higher than anything I had read and yet, somehow, it still seemed very low.

We all turned to Mom, the woman who had been paralyzed by medical anxiety for as long as I could remember.

"Well now — that's almost half!" She said with vigor. The mood instantly lightened. Mom was ready to face it, fight it, and do what we needed of her. This was all for us. *Everything my mother did was all for us.*

***

The next morning after I wore my new Easter jewelry and my grandma Marney had given me a little bunny, my dad came upstairs and told my sister to turn her hairband music off. It had been shaking the walls. That wasn't unusual. She turned it down.

"All the way off." he said as he crested the staircase. My other sister and I came into the hallway without anybody telling us to.

"Oh no." my middle sister squeaked under her breath. She had just turned 14, somewhere between a kid and not wanting to be a kid. I looked up to her and felt my heart jump upon hearing her scared.

I don't remember what words he said, but I remember my oldest sister folding her face into her hands. Her hair was already curled and big for school. As my dad hugged her, my middle sister and I sat in silence. In shock or unsure what it all meant. We were stuck somewhere between being kids and not understanding enough, and being kids and understanding all too well.

It was less than an hour to the start of school. Mom and Dad let us decide if we wanted to go. It was a quick and hard no from me and my middle sister. My oldest sister was never one to turn down a little extra attention, so she soldiered on.
We didn't do a lot that day, but it was sunny. That bright school day sun again. It seemed to be losing its shine. I'd give up the elusive bright midday sun just to go back to normal.

It was quiet in our house during those daylight hours. I wonder now if Mom had wished we'd gone to school. She had a lot to do. And yet, probably wished she'd had more to keep her busy. But my mom didn't complain.

My middle sister and I watched Regis and Kathy Lee. They didn't seem as funny as they had on Christmas break. At some point, we turned the tv off. That didn't happen much in our house – it was on whether anyone was watching it or not. Background noise, I guess. I sat in the sunroom in a white wicker chair that didn't rock. The cushion was stiff and uncomfortable, but I curled my feet onto it anyway. We had just added that room onto the house the year before. We called it the "sunroom". Its walls were windows; they let in a lot of light and looked out over the playhouse my grandma Marney and Gramps built. I didn't go out on it that day.

The next day, we found ourselves 20 miles away in the company of my grandmother's sister and several of the women she'd raised, including my mom. In tow were my middle sister and I. We were in the downtown that had a few women's dress shops. We were searching for an outfit for her to be buried in. At 9 years old, and still today, I wonder why then? Without a doubt, I know my grandmother would've wanted to be laid to rest in something she already had, something sensible, something free. Maybe it was a ploy to give my Gramps the day to himself at home. He'd had a *lot* of visitors lately, maybe he needed peace. Maybe all the women just needed something to do with themselves. All I remember is that there were a lot of opinions that day, mine included.

Though my opinion of her outfit wasn't required, she looked very nice lying in-state at the funeral home. It was curious to me. She just looked like she was sleeping. Sleeping in a nice, mint green suit in a shiny wooden casket surrounded by flowers. She mostly looked like herself. I spent most of the day taking peeks at her. I watched her chest closely, watching for it to rise and fall. Though a few times I let my mind trick me, it kept still. It didn't feel real even though I could actually see her body. If I hadn't seen it, we'd be years behind in my understanding. So I suppose it was necessary. I thought of all the days she lay just like that in her hospital bed in the living room or even before she was sick. Every movie we watched, at home or in the theater, she took a little nap. I could curl up next to her and she'd be asleep almost immediately, long before the plot of the movie had been revealed. I spent that evening watching all these mourners tell stories of my grandmother; stories filled with laughter and tears, sweet small moments, and glimmers of who she was. Turns out, she had a whole other life before me. Who knew?

My teacher came through the receiving line towards the end of the night. It had been a long night of hugs from strangers. I smelled like a thousand different perfumes. In the midst of all those people, I felt lonely. My teacher's face was a welcome sight. Mrs Summers. She brought me a pencil case and a balloon. In my 9-year-old head, she was there for me alone. Boy, was I glad to see someone I recognized, someone who wasn't there to steal my Gramps away or make him cry more. In reality, she knew my grandmother from her time as a teacher, but I didn't care about that then. It felt really special.

On the day of the funeral, I was glad for the sanctuary of our house. Close to my Gramps, but far from the chaos that all the people in that house were bringing. When I'm grieving, I get grumpy, I guess. At least that day I did. Amid all the people, my Gramps felt far away. He must've needed them there. I just needed him.

16

After nearly a month of time in the hospital and many false alarms of going home, Mom was finally back at home. My childhood home. Dad pulled the car into the driveway, next to the black stained sign that my grandfather made. The sign read "Orchard Hill" and squeaked when the wind blew it back and forth under the lamppost.

My mother is laced through every fiber of that home, deep down through the roots of the apple trees. Her mark is in every shade of blue paint because blue was her favorite. Her stories haunted every corner of the landscape- from the huge shrubs that covered most of the front of the house to the western sunsets that cascaded over the cow fields. My mother made that home, in every sense.

I knew she would regain her lost strength here. This is where she raised her daughters and loved her husband best. This is where she spent the last 12 hours of her energy (before she got really sick) wrapping presents for her grandkids. This is where she fed the birds and stray cats every single morning for 40 years. *Home.*

It was a deep sigh of relief to have Mom back where she belonged. We had a plan, despite it changing by the hour. Just being home made everything feel like there was a way forward, and for maybe even a second or two we could forget about the cancer that was consuming our thoughts.

Lists of medications, schedules, and checklists covered the kitchen table. The fridge was loaded with foods that would entice her to eat more. I tried desperately to combine mom's favorite snack brownies with cancer fighting ingredients. I did well to waste a lot of ingredients for something nobody ate. It was my way of "doing something" for her while I was at my home trying to take care of things there too. I was juggling a lot of balls, but I wasn't keeping them all up. Many days, the balls were all on the ground and I sat among them, searching the internet in tears trying to cure cancer real quick.

It had been a few weeks since she got sick, but now Mom was getting around best by using a wheelchair. She hated it, but it was necessary. And she hated it was necessary. We found great excitement in small victories daily. Maybe she ate more than we anticipated or stayed awake longer than the day before. Some days, we had to dig deep to find the victories. They never came easily.

Sam built a ramp to the door of Orchard Hill so Mom could be transported more easily to her frequent doctor's appointments and occasional trips back to the hospital. While we were inside the warm house, he put the whole thing up himself like a one-man Amish barn raising. The temperature was in the single digits that day. Mom didn't want anyone to see her sick. She didn't want those memories to haunt her grandchildren. My husband could've warmed up in the car that day, but he wanted to make sure it all got done perfectly and safely for her. He wanted to do something for her —she was a mother to him too.

Back when Sam and I started dating, I told her everything about him. He was putting himself through college and working, without the support of his family. She went grocery shopping for him, so he'd have food to eat. She found a kindred spirit in him as another member of our family that didn't have a father. He was estranged from his since childhood. Her father left when she was a baby and she never saw him again. The rest of us had grown up rather spoiled by siblings and easy answers to "who are your parents?". Their bond was what kept him in the freezing cold that day so he could do something for the woman who had done so much for him.

I told myself that she had enough forward movement to see hope. I took each moment of clarity or appetite as a building block that tomorrow would be a stronger day for her. She fought food down her throat, took her medicine like a champ, and watched a whole lot of HGTV. She'd wake up some mornings and, just for a moment, forget she was sick. I'll never forget the look on her face when she shared this with me — it was devastating.

Of course, we also had lighter moments of arguing over which wedding dress a tv bride should choose and talked about Chip and JoJo like they were close personal friends.

One late afternoon, as I gave my mother a sponge bath and washed her hair —I contemplated how grateful I was to be caring for her. As the shampoo poured over her smooth brown locks — I took the moment in. Caring for the woman who had washed my hair as a baby, held it back when I was sick, and patted it while I labored with my own children. *I knew I would remember this full circle moment.*

Mom was embarrassed. She kept saying how I didn't have to do any of that, but I wanted to. Mom was always the caregiver, to everyone in her life. This was my chance. We treated it like a spa day. The scalp massage to shampoo her hair allowed her to relax even for a second. The smell of lavender filled the house. I used lavender lotion to rub her feet in hopes it would help calm her anxiety just a little. Though Mom always liked having her feet rubbed, they were turning black now. They hurt from the chemo — just like everything else.

Rubbing lotion on her feet gave her temporary relief. I rubbed her feet as long as I could. For her spa bath day, the lavender mixed with the smell of eucalyptus, and we joked in a French accent. Mom always laughed at our jokes even when they weren't funny. She didn't have the energy that day, but I kept going because I could tell she wanted to laugh. I know God is always present. But there are times in life that His presence feels palpable, physical. The room was filled with peace and our senses filled with lavender. As I worked to keep her feet warm through various means, I remembered back to my childhood the old-man-on-the-porch, whose hands had been warmed by my mother's kindness when I was in the fourth grade.

***

It was the year my grandma Marney died. My mom had started working at my elementary school and, most days, arrived just a little bit late. The air started to turn cold, and the holidays were around the corner. We kept Thanksgiving mostly the same. I'm positive there were some decorations that couldn't be found or a missing recipe because there are just some things that people take with them. But as a nearly 10-year-old, I didn't notice. It was uneventful, something that everyone probably was grateful for after so many *events*.

My birthday was a week and a half after Thanksgiving.

My mom let me have a "friends" birthday party that year, and I believe my sisters are still jealous of this to this day. Each of us girls were allowed 2 friends parties – one in 1st grade, one in 5th grade.

Maybe it's because I'm the baby and my mom gave up on not spoiling us (although I never did get to go to that Boyz II Men concert so I wouldn't say completely spoiled). Maybe it was because my sisters were older, so she let me "catch up" with them a little so I wasn't left out.

Looking back, though, maybe it changed when my grandma Marney died. I'm sure she saw the void that she knew couldn't be filled, but she could try anyway. So maybe 4 friends over for presents and a surprise trip to McDonalds didn't fix it, but it wouldn't hurt anything either.

I rocked a light up reindeer sweatshirt and played board games with my girls. My BFFs. I'm sure I signed the invites LYLAS because we abbreviated everything before texting even existed. That's "love ya like a sister" in case you were wondering.

Perhaps whatever reason propelled that extra birthday also propelled the Halloween parties and swimming parties I had over the years, though never before 4th grade.

176

Everybody feels sorry for December babies because there's a rumor they might feel overlooked. I can say with total honesty — I have never felt overlooked. I have always loved the twinkling Christmas tree in the background of every birthday cake. I love the double wish lists. I love tinsel and sparkle and red and green.

As we got closer to Christmas, my mom and I conspired to leave a present for the old man on his porch. His waves continued as the air grew colder. His legs were covered with a blanket, but his hands were still bare. Mom took me to the store and let me pick out a gift set with a nice pair of gloves and a matching scarf.

Attached to the set was a little gift card, on which we carefully scripted "From Santa". We made a special trip past the house in the afternoon, when he'd be inside from his morning porch time. My hands shook as I raced to the porch and quickly but carefully set it up so he could easily see it on his porch swing.

My 10-year-old self desperately wanted to see him find it. I had the self-serving desire to feel good about the little thing we had done. But Mom said we didn't need to see him find it. She said we'd just know ourselves we had brightened someone's day. The very next day, he sat under his blanket in the chilly morning air with a fresh new set of gloves on his hands and scarf around his neck.

And then, on some unrecognized morning, we saw him, not knowing what it was — the last time. *We pass by all these recognized strangers, who end up being integral to our memories and we don't even know their names, or when will be the last time we see them.*

***

As I worked to keep Mom's feet warm and we tried to find some semblance of a "new" normal with cancer a presence in our lives, Sam and I continued worshipping Sunday mornings at our church in our town. Someone stayed with Mom at home while Dad continued preaching at the little country church where I opened my eyes under the waters of baptism.

One Sunday, as the lyrics to "Mansions Over the Hilltop" rose from my lips, I couldn't contain inexplicable tears any longer. I was grateful to be towards the back of the church. It was the last hymn of the service, and I planned to tuck and roll out of that building without making eye contact as fast as my body would carry me. I knew that containing the tears wasn't in the cards that morning — the energy to stop them had been used up in the middle-of-the-night internet searches to cure cancer. I wasn't even sure what it was about that song that stabbed right at my heart, but I doubt it took much.

Maybe I was allowing myself to consider that Mom was closer to that home than I'd ever let myself consider before. Maybe I selfishly couldn't let myself consider it before. I felt Sam's hand squeeze mine, but I couldn't look over. I snuggled our sleeping August on my lap tighter and planned to use her as a cover as soon as we were ready to leave. As the announcements finished, I turned to leave and the lady behind me put her hand on my shoulder. I hadn't made it out. *Dang.*

"Are you okay?" she asked, with a gentle shoulder pat.

"My mom is sick." I didn't want to explain anymore. I didn't want to say the word "cancer" aloud. I didn't want any more stories about someone they knew who died or didn't die or was cured or wasn't cured. I was overwhelmed.

"I'm so sorry, honey." She finished up, letting me go.

Just the right thing. I wonder if she knew she said just the right thing. *Sometimes the work God does in others is so small, you might almost miss it.*

I felt the arms of my oldest sons around my shoulders on either side of me as we scurried out to the car. Both boys were shorter than me and their arms stretched upwards to reach me as I carried their baby sister in my arms. She started to wake, but I patted her hair to gently lull her back to be my sleeping shield. The boys were like a SWAT team, ready to avoid eye contact and change our route if it seemed like someone might want to shake hands. We'd shake hands another day.

None of us *really* knew what was coming, but somehow God was preparing us little by little. I knew my boys shouldn't have to be comforting or helping me. It was supposed to be the other way around. Sometimes it was. Other times, like the walk from church to the car that day, I saw them maturing right before my eyes.

My children had faced, talked about, been surrounded by death their entire lives. Keely's life, and therefore, Keely's death affected each of them. Grief isn't something you get over, I'm afraid. There is no softening the finality of saying goodbye to someone you love no matter how many times or how many ways you've said it before. Sometimes an arm around the shoulders is all you can do and, very often, exactly what is necessary.

God accompanied me on the hour-long drive back and forth to help care for my mom. Sometimes I spoke to Him aloud. Sometimes I tried to drown the whole world out with music. Sometimes I called Sam to bring me comfort the way he always can. Some days that hour went fast. Other days, the drive felt endless. Some days I didn't really remember making the drive at all.

Those drives back and forth continued, filled with black coffee and hopeful prayer. I searched for a sign in any random occurrence – lots of bunnies on the drive up must mean good luck! Red sky at night, I'll take it. Anything that seemed hopeful. I noticed that when I wore my bright pink sweatshirt, we always got bad news. I didn't consider that we got bad news all the other days too. Regardless, into the back of the closet went that pink sweatshirt. *I haven't worn it since.*

The hospital trips were frequent and seemed to be getting shorter, which I took as a good sign. We would take turns taking her in for chemo. My turn went something like this:

Her numbers were too low for chemo. *Pray.*
"Should we try anyway?", I'd ask. *Pray.*
They'd take her numbers again. Still too low. *Pray.*
Proceed with chemo. *Pray.*
Pray.

Pray fervently. Pray frantically.

***

The chemo was pumped into my mom's veins as she slept propped up in her chair. In the moment she was occupied, I became overwhelmed and stepped out of the room. I didn't want her to see me cry. I was the self-appointed but secretly unsure optimist — I didn't want her to see me uncertain.

As I gathered myself and my thoughts in the hallway, my mother's doctor was passing by. I didn't make eye contact, though. I was too busy settling my own thoughts. However, I noticed as he stopped in front of me.

"I wish there was something I could do." He offered up. "I really do. I would do it for your family."

I searched his face for the confidence bordering on arrogance my daughter's surgeon had offered. His eyes were filled with compassion. I didn't want him to be certain, though. *I wanted him to be wrong.*

Without my response, he continued. "She's dying, though. I'm very sorry."

I stood in shock. I didn't say a word. I hadn't asked.

180

I DIDN'T ASK. I didn't want to know.

I narrowed and focused my eyes on this man I hadn't asked a question to but who was offering up an answer I didn't want to hear. Though I was taller than the doctor, I felt like the little girl shorter than the kitchen partition in my parents' house again.

***

At almost 9 years old, I was still shorter than the partition separating the dining room from the kitchen at Orchard HIll. As I rounded the corner, I heard "She's dying, Debs.". I stopped my high stepping and leaned into the wall, just in view of my parents. My white - blonde head of hair sunk into the wall. The words hung in the air. They were sitting at the kitchen table and stopped and turned to me. They hadn't known I was there — it was all over their faces. My mother's face was red from tears. My dad's face showed anguish at being unable to help. I knew my grandmother had been sick. But I hadn't considered she was *sick*. I hadn't asked. I didn't want to know.

***

The days I spent in my childhood home helping care for my mom started earlier and earlier. Armed with coffee and insomnia, I snuck in quietly in case Mom and/or Dad had been able to sleep. I lined up medicines, checked the times, cleaned the dishes, threw away tissues, and prayed the whole way through.

When Mom woke up, I rubbed her feet and we chatted. For a split second, we'd both enjoy the delight in her eyes when she saw me there. *The moment would end when she remembered why.* We talked those mornings the same way we had every morning for years. We talked about television shows, grandkids' interests, celebrity news, and any other silly thing that popped into our minds. The more tired Mom became from treatment, the shorter the conversations got.

181

I'd continue rubbing her feet because, even as she looked to be sleeping, it was light at best. Rubbing the lavender lotion on her feet was one of the very few things I could do to help at all.

On this Sunday morning, her feet were black and cold, but the rubbing helped. I was pumping the blood through her toes for her since they couldn't do it themselves.

It was bright that day despite winter sticking around. A red cardinal danced at the window of the living room Mom was resting in. When she'd get sore, we'd help her move around or flip her to the other side. Every movement needed help now, but her spirits were good. Good, but quiet. Mom couldn't see the cardinal from her angle, so I took a picture with my cell phone and showed her that way. Mom's beloved birds were coming to see her. We kept them fed just as she requested.

Years later, I found solace in the cell phone bird image—enveloping it into a photographic composite titled "Messenger from Heaven". My youngest son, with his chubby freckled cheeks and shocked expression was photographed in my studio. He was holding a book. I composited that image next to a broken window and greenery from my parent's house. I painted a little scroll into that very bird's mouth. I painted over the screen in the image to highlight the red feathers and twinkle in his eye. The image was straight from my imagination and laced with layers of meaning. My own personal therapy has been to thread these moments into my work, like easter eggs only I can see. If you're in my little circle, I'll share them with you too.

There were two rare occurrences. The first being that all three of us girls were there together. We had been adjusting our schedules so that someone was always there, which meant we weren't there together. I couldn't tell you the last time it had been just my two sisters, parents, and I in the house on Orchard Hill without a son-in-law or grandchild in sight — at least a dozen years, probably more.

The second rare occurrence was that it was so very quiet. The television stayed off that day. Even as a child, the tv was on as background noise. The Food Network or infomercials filled the air when no one was watching. I kept asking Mom if she wanted it on, but she insisted she didn't. We all held our breath when it seemed like she might be able to sleep. It was too quiet. Every clatter of a dish or heavy sigh was heard and felt by everyone.

"You sure, Mom?" asking about the tv for me more than her. She was sure, though.

My oldest sister went home first. She lived in town and spent the bulk of hours in caring. Since we were there, she could go home to be with her children who'd been missing her during this time.

Watching her work staying busy reminded me so much of our Nana. She grieved the way our mother's mother had when Keely died. She stayed busy. She found work for herself in the dishes, the vacuum, the bathroom sink. She filled the air with Lysol and made sure the baseboards weren't dusty. She scrubbed the travel coffee cup I brought with me and forgot every time. A farmer's wife, she found comfort in completed work. *It was the ghost of my mother's mother, present in the busyness of grief.*

My middle sister left later in the afternoon. She was the visitor. When she came, she'd sit by Mom and chat. Our mother wanted nothing more than to visit with us, as simple as that. She loved just chatting. In addition to visiting us, Mom always liked to hear my sisters and I visit.

She never had the sibling relationships that my sisters and I were blessed with. Blessed with, despite the fights over sweaters and the phone growing up. Blessed with, despite deeper differences as adults. *Blessed with despite what we were facing now in our mother's cancer diagnosis.* Blessed with, despite maybe never really knowing each other at all. Blessed with, even if we fell apart after my mom was gone. My middle sister had the gift of being able to lighten a room, even as heavy as this one most days.

The next day was Monday, so I knew I wouldn't be able to come back. Sam had to be at work that day, so I'd stay a little while longer this evening. Before she was sick, Mom would make sure we were all on the road in time to get back to our homes before it was dark out. This was especially true on the cold evenings of winter. While she was sick, however, she didn't mention it anymore. She hoped for a few more minutes together — *so did we.*

The sun was falling behind the cow pasture out the western bay window. The cold was starting to bite more as shadows took over the sun. Mom seemed settled and comfortable. She had a hard time getting comfortable the night before this, but she seemed to be resting well now. I weaned off rubbing her feet to keep her comfortable the way I would've while putting one of my babies to sleep. I didn't want to disturb her. I crept into Dad's den to let him know I'd be heading home soon. He was working on something and asked if I'd stay a few more minutes with Mom until he finished.

I returned to Mom to see her lift her eyes towards me. I felt bad I had left the room while she was still awake. I know she liked the peace and quiet, but she also wanted us near.

"Hey, ma. How are you feeling?" I asked, sometimes still feeling like the 8-year-old that followed her around. I wanted her to have a burst of energy, ready to take on more chemotherapy in just two days. Every dose she could battle through gave me hope that she'd turn a corner soon. *We just needed a good corner.*

She gave me a smile and patted my hand. Before even answering me, Dad knelt next to her and said "Debs, I'm going to have an ambulance come." And she patted his hand too. She shook her head in agreement.

I backed up a little with the distinct feeling I had missed something important.

"What?" I asked Dad, afraid I spaced out on him telling me something. *Something within me stopped me from asking any more questions, and something stopped Dad from answering at all.*

He rushed off to make phone calls and I sat on the floor next to Mom lying on the couch. I held her hand. She seemed pretty good. I tried to understand why the sudden rush. I tried to understand why the ambulance. *Why now?* I began to operate under the assumption they were both so tired that maybe another bad night seemed like too heavy a load to bear. *More eyes on her at the hospital was probably a good idea.*

As we waited for the ambulance to arrive, Dad prepared the house to be empty for the night. A lady from church also arrived to check in.

Mom was very clear from the beginning – no visitors. She was focused on her health, focused on us. She didn't want her grandkids —the light of her life — to see her sick. If she couldn't see them, she didn't want to see anyone.

While there was still time for me to stop her near the door and preserve Mom's sanctuary by the western window, I bent down quickly to ask if Mom was okay with this visitor. She very much was. I was surprised, but also relieved. This was a woman who had worked in nursing for a long time and had the spirit of an angel. I was prepared to be a bouncer for Mom, but it wasn't necessary this day.

She came in, spoke softly to Mom, gave me a hug, and brought a peaceful presence with her. She agreed with Dad that the hospital was the right move.

Eventually, after the sun was long gone, we waited to get Mom settled into a room at the hospital. In the meantime, they decided to do another scan on her. I was excited. The impatient woman that I am, I wanted to know that all this work was paying off. I wanted Mom to hear good news. I wanted all her pain and suffering to be worthwhile. I texted Sam and told him I wasn't sure now what time to expect me home. I kept him updated on the changing plans and changing hopes. *My husband has far more patience than I do.*

We were still in the small room of the hospital where you wait for your real room. Mom had been scanned and we overheard the clerk at the desk making phone calls about her. Dad and I made eye contact with one another and, without a word, moved closer to the door. We silently willed everything and everyone else in the hospital to silence so we could take in the words over the phone that weren't meant for us to hear.

The scans showed that chemo was working against the tumor in the kidney. It was the origin. *That had to be good, right?* I scoured the internet for answers and waited for the doctor to tell us the good news. I held Mom's hand and ignored the bumps that now covered her arms from under her skin. We weren't even sure what they were, but there were too many symptoms now to consider each one individually — symptoms of cancer, symptoms of chemo.

Maybe this was the corner we needed. Dad was too nervous to take any of it in as good news. He tried to stifle my excitement with logic. *I would have none of that.*

"Don't say anything, Chooch." Dad whispered out of earshot from Mom, who was sleeping as well as she slept at all anymore.

"I won't, Dad. I know, we have to wait." I knew that information wasn't meant for us, and I knew it probably wasn't as good as I was feeling at that moment.

I clung to something being good news. Anything. We gave the bad news our sleep at night, so I could at least give hope a few hours now.

Mom was given a room later that night and I made it home just before day break. Everyone was settled. I shared the information with Sam over coffee just a few hours later. He held the same reserved skepticism that Dad had. *What were they seeing that I was missing? What was I allowing or even hoping to miss?* I didn't let myself think about it too long.

The good news I was awaiting after eavesdropping never came.

17

Our final hope was the hospital where I live. They had doctors there daily— including specialty doctors. There they had a whole team of experts. There, we'd get answers. There, we'd get help, but the beds were full. There was no room in the hospital quite yet. I considered all the reasons a bed would become available, and I prayed for a miraculous recovery rather than the alternative.

What ended up happening was longtime clients of mine pulled strings to help move things along. They were scheduled to have a family photo shoot with me just a few days later. I received an email from my client after just a few hours in the new hospital rescheduling. She wanted me to focus on my family, not hers, for the time being. She'd see me soon. *Everyone seemed to know something I wouldn't allow myself to know.* With this knowledge, she gave me the grace I needed to comfortably stay close to mom. *I was so grateful.*

As they loaded Mom into the ambulance, I headed out to my car. I basked in a freshly made memory of mom. While we were waiting in Mom's hospital room, Sam texted me a silly picture of Beckham. Our youngest son was covered in temporary tattoos, and he was making the face of a wrestling champion. I chuckled to myself and shared it with Mom on my phone. She let out a genuine, full belly laugh. We both clung to that second for longer than we would have just weeks before. *I revisit that moment still.* We were driving separately and moving at different rates but would reunite at the hospital an hour away. I wasn't more than 15 minutes out of town when the ambulance in my rearview mirror flew past me. I tried to get a glimpse to see if it was them, but they passed me in a blink. I thought it had to be them so, for a moment, I tried to keep up. *Later I found out Mom was terrified in the ambulance, and they feared they may lose her on the way.*

Once we all arrived, we were back in a little room waiting for a regular room and this time, Mom had a roommate. My sisters and I listened through the curtain as they explained that the neighbor was going to hospice. We made eye contact with one another and pitied the family receiving that news. *It was just hours later that we would hear the same, only there would be no time for hospice.*

The new doctor was a specialist in Mom's specific cancer. The best around. Instead of hope, she gave us the pity we doled out just hours before.

The new doctor explained that while the chemotherapy was showing slight improvement in Mom's cancer, it wasn't enough. Whether it was chemo or cancer, Mom's body was shutting down. Mom appeared to be sleeping, but I could see that she was hearing this. *I didn't want her to hear this.* I wanted her to know I hadn't given up, diagnosis be damned.

"But, if she rests this weekend and regains energy, we could try chemo again, right?" I paused while the doctor looked at me like I was speaking another language. Her face said, without words, that I wasn't understanding her.

"Even if it were a miracle, that's what we'd do, right?" God could do it for Mom. I know He could. I prayed He would. I prayed that Mom could hear my hope for her.

The doctor reluctantly agreed with my illogical hope for the weekend.

"Are you okay with all of that, Mom?" I wanted the doctor to know Mom heard it all. The doctor was speaking like she couldn't.

"Yes, babe." Mom answered, opening her eyes only a bit.

"Oh." The doctor said, barely audibly.

Doctors know a lot. But I knew my mother. I also knew in that moment if we had come to a doctor more prepared for my mother's type of cancer, they wouldn't have treated her at all. She would've been sent home to die. I knew she wanted to try— not for her — but for us. For our peace of mind. I found tremendous gratitude for the doctor in my hometown at that moment. He had been willing to let us try. *He allowed us hope when, truly, there was none.*

My unwarranted hope and I waited alongside everyone else who seemed more in touch with reality for my mom's private room.

She finally got situated on the cancer floor. We didn't see another patient or visitor the entire time we were there. They probably wouldn't have wanted to see us either. We were a reminder of the bed that would be vacant soon for all the wrong reasons.

I remembered back to my long wheelchair ride through the maternity ward, empty-armed. I assumed at that time that everybody could tell from looking at me something was wrong, even what was wrong. In the hallway of the cancer unit, that familiar feeling crept in and my face glowed hot.

I texted Sam to fill him in. He assured me the kids were fine. He assured me I could stay as long as I needed. He seemed to know something I hadn't told him. *He seemed to know something I hadn't let myself hear yet.*

Mom struggled to find positions free of pain after riding in the ambulance. Rubbing her feet didn't help anymore. They were so cold. Turning her side-to-side didn't help anymore, but we tried anyway. She relied on morphine to comfort her body that was giving way.

She seemed resigned. She had known all along this was coming. She had a good life. She had a good life, I repeated to myself the way Mom had — with more vigor.

When I was a little girl, I rode along with Mom to all kinds of things— my sister's band concerts, my dad's sporting events, theme parks, craft shows. We'd ask each other questions — sometimes silly, sometimes serious. I never felt younger than in that hospital room while asking my mom those last few questions. While she slept, I considered all the questions I had forgotten to ask.

I was relieved to know how she cut her toast into triangles the way her grandmother had and always mixed brownies with a wooden spoon, so it was easier to lick the batter from the bowl. I would take this knowledge with me. I considered all the little things that would die alongside her, all the things we'd never know now. I wondered about the tiny moments that were special to her, but she hadn't thought to share. *It was too late now.*

"Are you scared, Mom?" I asked. I was scared to ask. I wasn't sure I wanted the answer.

She shook her head yes. *Oh no.*

"Are you scared for you, Mom?" I asked, confident she wasn't. My mother was never loud with her faith, but it was easily seen in her actions.

She shook her head no.

"Are you scared for us, Mom?" I paused. Her energy was escaping her.

She shook her head yes and her face looked pained. I wished I could reassure her more, but I was scared for us too. She was our anchor. Tears poured from my face onto her shoulder.

"We'll take care of each other, Mom, just like you taught us. I promise." I promised her as my dad stroked the hair on top of her head.

"We'll do our best." I tried to hide my own fears, but it wasn't working. If I tried to hide something from Mom, she'd know it. *Even as she lay dying.*

She motioned her hands towards me and summoned all the energy left in her body. I leaned over her for one last hug. It was a good, tight hug. She held on to me longer than I expected. I was grateful for that. As her energy slipped away, I could tell she wanted something, so I began the questions that we always fell back to.

"Do you want Dad to sing to you?" I asked. I don't know what made me ask that question, but she shook her head yes.

My dad's side eye told me he wasn't expecting that, nor did he think he had the ability at that moment. He found it though and softly sang "Sweet Hour of Prayer" as my mom relaxed into the bed. It called her from the world of care to seize the everlasting prize. The air lifted as the room was filled with a hymn of just the right words. I asked Dad months later how he chose such a perfect hymn on the spur of the moment like that. He didn't remember choosing, really — it just came to him. *I figured as much.*

We spent 41 hours in that room. The only window looked out onto a concrete wall. No light could creep in, but we pulled the shades closed just in case. We sat among dozens of empty Styrofoam coffee cups that stacked up by the hour, along with the tear-streaked tissues.

We sent texts to pray, and we knew people wanted to see her. They wanted to talk to her one more time or give her a hug one more time. People loved my mom and needed one last moment with her. But those were moments for them. We knew her wishes. My mother spent her entire life doing things for other people. These were supposed to be her moments and she wanted them to be private. She made that very clear before she gave her last, tight hug and before the final words left her breath.

As I sat by my mother, holding her hand, I was grateful pain seemed to be losing its grip on her. She relaxed into the morphine that became more and more necessary. She focused her eyes straight ahead of her, up towards the ceiling and whispered "not yet" as she blew air through pursed lips.

The last 16 hours were silent. Heartbeats, ever so slowly. Breaths, ever so deeply. Time moved far too fast. In those final hours, a friend of my dad's stopped in to pray with us. The gesture was kind, but the timing was wrong. We had no idea someone might just… walk in. His stay was brief and uncomfortable, but it was enough to send out texts to let others know that we weren't prepared for visitors. We tried to be respectful that others needed *something*, but this couldn't be about them. *Let this be about her and her wishes, just this once.*

We had been too polite. The urgency in our messages had been lost and we didn't know until a relative walked into my mother's room of goodbyes without warning. We tried to shield her failing body because she didn't want to be seen. Just as her mother didn't want her body lying in a casket in view of everyone, my mother didn't want to see anyone. But here came someone anyway because it was about what they needed, not her. I tried to extend grace, but I didn't find it that day. *Or the next day either.*

More texts went out with more blunt language that surely couldn't be ignored. We knew of one car en route to the hospital and returned home. We were grateful for the respect even if it had been forced. We whispered jokes about a trap door or security detail. We drank more coffee and held her hands.

At some point in those final hours, my prayers shifted. They had been so selfish. My prayers had been for a miracle cancer cure. I wanted my mom. I felt far too young to be saying goodbye to my mom. I didn't think how if she'd gone into remission, she would've been chased by a dark cloud of worry that the cancer was coming back. I didn't think how tired she was. I didn't think about how her final thoughts weren't fear for herself but worry for us. Her thoughts were always of us. *I didn't think about how maybe she was ready to be called Home.*

My prayers shifted to peace for her. My prayers shifted to rest for her body and mind. My prayers became hope for a kind of comfort and understanding for all of us that surpasses what we're capable of alone. My prayers shifted. I don't think there's a place on earth that feels closer to God than where He's bringing someone Home.

I watched the clock and searched for meaning in the numbers. Did one mean more than the others? I wasn't even sure what day it was. The space between words among my sisters, dad, and I grew distant as fatigue and deep sadness took over the room. There was no wind or lightning clap. Nothing changed from one moment to the next except my mother was gone from this world.

We held our breath waiting to see if she'd muster one or two more, but there would be no more breaths from my mother's lungs. Who she was and what she was — now within each of us. Her work was done while ours was just beginning. Works of the heart. Works of grieving.

Peace for her.

One of the nurses told me that it's rare for a mother to die with all her children by her side. It seemed very right for my mom, who had made us her life's work. *That is a luxury I already know I won't have.*

We left the hospital in midafternoon. The sun was bright and high in the sky. The rays of light burnt into my eyes as I walked out the front door. It was the first natural light any of us had seen in 41 hours. It was supposed to be dark out.

I wasn't prepared for the weather to do anything other than mirror my emotions. The air was crisp and cool, but the sun shouldn't be so bright, not in winter, especially not now. The hospital had been dark and gray. The smells had been of cleaning supplies and cold metal. Going outside offered no comfort or warmth. The world should have been heartbroken right alongside me, but the sun beamed brightly, nonetheless.

My sisters, Dad, and I just kind of *left*. We left to go to our homes. We left to try to rest after the days on end spent in vigilance of death. It felt weird to not have an agenda to plan for. We all just went our separate ways, not ready to share with the world how ours had changed but it would become necessary soon.

I went home to Sam and the kids. They were so excited to see me, and I was about to ruin it for them. I thought maybe they'd know just by looking at me. I thought maybe I wouldn't have to say it. Part of me hoped they wouldn't understand, but a bigger part of me knew they would.

I did have to say it. They didn't want to let themselves hear it any more than I wanted to say it. Even our little August, who had her second birthday while Mom was in the first weeks of her diagnosis, cried. These children had faced death in one way or another most days of their lives, but there's no getting used to it.

Death comes to us in different forms, with different surprises, and with new heartbreak every time. We piled onto the couch in a puddle of grief. I melted into the arms of my husband, whose heart was broken too. I saw him cry for the second time in our lives. There, for the first time in days — I slept.

I awoke just before bedtime, my body not quite ready to let me rest too long. It was time to make phone calls. They were to the same people I had called just five weeks before, but with very different news now. I wasn't ready to make these calls, but I remembered the visitors we'd been unprepared for and how word could spread quickly through social media. I didn't want the people most special to Mom to find out anything from somewhere else.

I made many calls that evening, but Mom's cousin was the one I remember most. She had badly wanted Mom to call her. She was halfway across the country, but she and Mom never went that long without talking.

I remembered back to Mom sitting in the kitchen on the chair beneath the yellow phone with a long cord. Mom twisted her fingers through the cord and back out while she caught up with her. In between phone calls, they wrote letters to each other. They never allowed too much time to pass. I knew her daughters wanted to be there if I had to make that call, but I worried that another family member would get to her first.

She knew before I said a word. I tried to force out words over a mumble and through tears, but she knew anyway. She let out a terrible scream. It was the sound of her heart breaking. I wished I could have hugged her.

The next day, I found myself going back to the funeral home where I felt like I had become a usual customer. We went to the same funeral home — into the same room I'd been in 11 years earlier for my daughter's funeral. Now here I was, in a room that I felt so old in before, feeling so very young now.

The kind old man that had helped us so much was gone. It was a younger man now, less distinguished but still warm and welcoming. We checked all the necessary boxes and answered questions that would fulfill my mom's obituary. We had messed up making good on the promise to make sure her death was private, but we could fulfill the remaining of her requests now. *We had learned lessons from her mother's funeral that we were determined not to repeat.*

She wanted to be cremated. She didn't want her body displayed for the funeral. She wanted Dad to go back to Disney and the beach with us. We could do that easily. It was what she wanted, and this was for her. I spent the next nights creating photo gifts for her grandchildren to be displayed at the funeral home and then for each of them to take home. I printed big photographs of her to display as well. Now that part was for us. My mom would not have wanted her picture displayed anywhere if she could avoid it.

There was one picture I took of her at the beach, though, that she didn't hate. She was in her happy place, listening to the waves crash, smelling the salt in the air, and the peace was all over her face. She would've been okay with that one and it embodied her, I decided.

She would have loved that after the funeral home meeting, my dad, sisters, and I had appetizers at a pizza place. She would have loved that her grandchildren were getting presents at her funeral. She would have loved we were all together. She would've gotten such a kick out of our laughter going through photographs, but she would've been irritated if we didn't put the huge albums back in the shelves just right. I couldn't narrow down the hundreds of photos of mom.

We had to include all the ones of her and dad growing up together. They were still growing up together, even as they raised us. We had to include her with each of us girls, on all the vacations, in the pool, with her grandkids, at the beach, at Disney. We had to include all those precious happy moments that were a part of her. We had to include them all because they were all we were going to get. All the happy things in the world couldn't touch the peace she was surrounded by, though, and we were left to fathom it. We clung with both fists to the hope that only Christ can offer. *Our desperation for help turned into gratitude for hope over time.*

I searched high and low for funeral clothes for my children. I distinctly remembered what I wore to my grandmother's funeral as a little girl. Jackie Kennedy-esque, I told myself. I didn't know if my kids would care, especially the boys, but just in case, I'd make it special. So much was out of my control, and this was something I could handle whether they cared or not. I looked into the eyes of the cashiers at each clothing store, wondering if they could tell just by looking at me. I wondered what story they were holding.

I pored myself into menial tasks that really didn't matter, but I needed to focus hard on anything. My oldest sister and I bonded over preparing a room for after the funeral. *Why were we the ones doing this?* We pondered, grateful to have something to do. So many people said to "let them know" if we needed something, but we hadn't let them know. We cleaned up the house where Mom had received her care — the cups of water we hoped she'd drink, the tissues, the lavender lotion. We weren't all that used to cleaning up for ourselves at Orchard Hill. *It was time to grow up.*

During mom's visitation, I shook hundreds of hands, gave as many hugs, and found myself comforting people Mom had known years before and not since. I tried to fight the bitter resentment of people I had witnessed my mother give and give to continually for years, while receiving nothing in return. It spoke volumes about who she was but said plenty about the other party too.

I reminded myself that who she was wouldn't allow her daughter to steep in negative feelings towards anyone. So, I let it go. I had to let it go. We smelled a thousand different colognes and struggled to remember names and faces. We lined up in order... Dad, my oldest sister, my middle sister, and me. By the time everyone got to me, many had run out of things to say. I guess repeating "I'm sorry", "I'm sorry", "I'm sorry", "I'm sorry" gets redundant.

A man I'd known my whole life got to me in line, and judging by overhearing chatter, he had probably been in that line a couple of hours. My parents had gone to church with his family since before I was born. He was part of the group of families my parents shared New Years Eve with for more than 40 years.

They spent those years playing charades and Trivial Pursuit. They ate tiny hotdogs soaked in apricot baby food, a Midwest delicacy. Eventually, it was just them as all the children grew up and moved on to their own New Year's Eve parties. This had been the first year they'd miss. Mom was sick. Though others we barely knew, and Mom barely knew, had decided to jump the line — he hadn't. He and his family could have come right up to the front, but they didn't. They were content to spend that time in line and I was grateful for each of them. Their respect for my mother was noted. I assumed he had said all the usual stuff to my dad and sisters, but when he got to me, he put his hand on my shoulder and said two words.

"That's life." He gave me a pat as he continued past.

A smile spread across my face, *He's not wrong, I suppose.* That is life. Without life, there is no death and vice versa. I wonder if he walked away red-faced. Sometimes we all say things that come out wrong, but in the moment —I welcomed something new to hear. I considered it all quickly and turned to the next "I'm sorry." *Sometimes that left turn a conversation takes is exactly the side road that was needed.*

A referee from my high school soccer days came through the receiving line. He said he was glad to see me one time he didn't have to yellow card me. I was grateful for the laugh and glad to see the support my dad was receiving from his soccer colleagues.

"I didn't know she was sick." Many people said as they passed through the line. *Well, neither did we.* We soaked in stories of Mom as a young girl or feisty teenager. We listened about how she touched people's lives in church and work. We listened about how she cared for people when no one was watching. Like the old man and his warm gloves, my mom cared for people and didn't need them to notice. She didn't need to be seen. *But she was seen, even if only after.*

I wondered how many of these people told Mom how wonderful she was, or did they wait to tell her family? Had I told her how special she was? Did she believe me? I made mental notes of people I hadn't expected to see. I searched the crowds for people I was surprised to not see.

I looked at all the faces God placed before me those days. My faith is more than believing in God — it is seeing His hand in the people

He places in our lives. My faith is knowing He can, even when He doesn't. My faith is gratitude for those people surrounding me in the good and bad moments, in a thousand different ways. My faith holds me up when it's time to move on from them.

I stood before the room full of my mother's memories the next day and spoke to her life. My mother made our family her life's work. We were her priority – there was never any doubt of that. It was important to me to summon the strength to speak about her. This was all for her. She never wanted the spotlight or attention, but she deserved it. I made sure my words were short and meaningful. My words had to embody her whole life but ease the heaviness too. This was her Home-going. *We should rejoice for her while we grieve for our loss.*

Before it was my turn to go up and speak, I twisted a Kleenex back and forth between my fists. I didn't let the words of the hymns sink into my brain. I thought if I let those words in, my thoughts would be muddled with grief. I had to make myself focus so I could do what was right for her. *What if it was one of the last things I could do for her?* It had to be perfect.

Despite all the various losses I had endured, I hadn't learned grief doesn't really end. After I checked off all my marks for Keely's life and death, I was still her mother. I was tasked with her memory. After my mother's medication checklists were completed, I was still her daughter. *She would continue to live on— even in death.*

18

Three weeks later, almost to the day, I was on the receiving end of a phone call just like I'd been making less than a month earlier. My mother's beloved cousin, like a sister to her, who herself had wailed in grief at my mother's death — passed away. She died of complications from diabetes, but I think maybe a broken heart played a role too.

In the coming days, weeks, months after my mother's death, my father and sisters and I all had to find new relationships with each other. *We had to forge relationships that didn't funnel through the woman who had been the anchor to our family.* We started group texts that were initially schedules and facts but morphed into pictures of grandkids and funny memes.

Dad would call us and say it was an accident. The man had never called someone just to chat or check in. He hadn't needed to because Mom always handled that. He was learning how now. I learned to talk to my dad on the phone. We learned to have a real conversation, albeit a short one. We learned to visit each other. We learned to just check in or just say hi.

Like the baby fawns that stumbled through my parents' lawn on Orchard Hill in the springtime — we were working on getting our footing. Sometimes we failed, sometimes we made progress, but we had no choice, we had to keep trying. I felt like a grief veteran but was seen by my family as the baby still. I felt like I saw the end sooner than the others. Grief doesn't end. *It changes and adjusts over time, but once it joins you — it is always your companion.*

***

When I met Sam, I was in the process of letting go of the things in my life that no longer served me. I had so many different directions I could see myself going – politics, law, architecture, history, writing, soccer. I really wanted to buy old houses, renovate them, and resell them. This was before "flipping" houses had tv shows and before anybody did that in my hometown. I searched colleges close by for historic preservation — there weren't many options.

My mom and I toured many campuses, talked to many tour guides, and spent many hours considering my options. I could truly see myself passionate about a lot of different careers, so there was and wasn't pressure. It all came down to not wanting to leave home yet. I would follow in the footsteps of my sisters to the local university and stay home with my family.

My middle sister moved out and my oldest sister was set to get married my first week of college so it would be just me, mom, and dad. It kind of had been this way for a while, but now it would be official. I landed on art as my major because it felt broad enough that I wouldn't have to commit to one career yet. It felt like something I would enjoy despite not having taken any art classes in high school. *It also felt like a challenge because you can't fake art.*

It was pretty easy to fake most classes in high school. Even if I weren't interested in them, I could remember the information long enough to ace a test. Art was putting yourself out there in an exposed way and I liked the idea of some level of subjectivity. After my unchallenging high school years, I was more than ready to have a goal.

I went on a lot of first dates in college. When the simple gold cross necklace I wore would catch the light, they'd ask if I were okay with them being atheist/agnostic/unbeliever/ etc. and I'd always say "yes" because I didn't want to be judgy.

If I said yes, I didn't have to answer any hard questions about the Bible, about God, about myself. I took the easy way out. I took the coward's way out. I was the conservative Christian in art school. I wanted to stand out in a good way, but not too much. I didn't want to stand out so much that I was singlehandedly representing God Himself. I figured I could let my artwork speak for me. I'd have to make it powerful enough to put me on an island.

Despite my best efforts to be a loner, I did make friends my first year in college. I met some beautiful souls and had some unforgettable moments. Mixed in with the friendships and first dates, I saw Sam often. We had many mutual friends and spent nights at many of the same parties.

One winter Friday, I needed to take some photographs for a class I was in, but everybody had class at that time. It was unusual that I couldn't get someone to skip and come along with me. Surprisingly, Sam said he'd go. We called it a playdate and I picked him up in my white Mustang. It was 68 degrees outside despite being January in Indiana.

The top was down on my convertible. My blonde hair was twisted into dozens upon dozens of tiny braids and covered in a blue bandana. The jeans I wore were covered in paint from class and signatures from people I was in class with. I was banking on a future when one of them would become famous and I could sell my jeans. This was not a date, so I didn't dress the way I would have for a date. This was hanging out with someone who I shared many mutual friends with.

This boy who didn't sugarcoat anything in class was blunt out of class too. He asked me to change the music in my car from the "Of A Revolution" mix cd that I'd had on repeat for months. I not-so-politely refused. Then I turned it up. It wasn't a date, so I didn't need to be on my best behavior. We drove to trails on the outskirts of town.

I remember it as a quiet park where not many people walked the trails but, if you did, you might find a body. Trains went through the woods occasionally, which kept wildlife and peace from lingering. We joked about finding a crime scene and how contrived pictures of trains were. I took one anyway and explained how mine would be different — it wasn't.

The day before our "playdate" was the last day Sam and I spent apart.

Less than a year later, much to the dismay of his friends, he asked me to marry him. Six months after that, we became husband and wife and moved to Chicago. The nearest congregation that matched with my beliefs was in an area of the city where crime rates said I shouldn't be going alone.

This is how my husband began attending church with me, and eight years later he would be baptized back in the same country church baptistry I had opened my eyes in when I was 14. And now, the art that helped me meet my husband was helping me soothe my grief.

God loves a full circle moment.

***

Just as I had when Keely died, I drowned myself in my artwork after mom's passing. I found solace in photography and digital art that allowed me to wade through my grief. I created personal work for competition and for my own purposes. I found peace in a digital painting that showed my mom and my daughter reunited in the sweet by and by.

It bombed in an image competition, but my dad proudly displays it next to the globe that contains my mother's ashes. That is the best trophy I could have asked for.

I continued working on my bereavement project. It spanned two years by now. I chipped away at it and photographed a new family several times a year. It wasn't coming along quickly, but it was coming along.

Each time, just like the trips before, I'd upload the photographs and take some time to emotionally digest what I needed to do with them next. Each bereavement session I shot — I remembered back to when I backed up from the computer screen to see all six of our children together for the first time. I couldn't wait to give that moment to other families. *I felt immense pressure to do it right.*

I stood ankle deep in the waters of a creek talking to a fellow bereaved mother after I photographed her living children for my project. We had known each other for years, but only got to meet in person when it was time for this photograph. We didn't have a lot of time, but it was enough to squeeze in a real conversation that we both needed to have.

A red cardinal landed on a shrub nearby. I noticed it as a little wink from God. These little signs He sends us are reminders of His works. *They're everywhere.* Just as its bright red settled in against a lush green shrub, this brokenhearted mother asked a question.

"Aly, do you really believe we'll see them again?" she asked, with a quivering voice.

Before I even got any words out, tears filled her eyes. I could feel the presence of God in that moment. He's always there, of course, but when someone is desperately searching for Him within you, His presence is palpable. Sometimes, recognizing your role in others' lives is important too. Neither would be possible without God, without His word, or without His presence.

"I do. I know our babies are with Him. I know it." I didn't have more words to convince her. I didn't need to convince her. Her faith had to do that part. *I was glad it was a question I could answer with certainty.*

Hiraeth is a Welsh word that means "homesickness for a place to which you cannot return, a place that perhaps no longer exists". As soon as I discovered the word, I knew it would be the title of the bereaved siblings project I'd been poring my heart into for years.

At the time the opening was set, it had been four years since the first frames were shot. Nineteen families participated, but I couldn't just let it be an odd number.

Since it had been so long, I put a period on that project by creating a second image of all six of my children. This time, Keely would have been thirteen years old.

After Mom died, I showed a lot of my work to Dad because it was born of grieving Mom. For the Hiraeth images, not sharing the images with the families for four years nearly drove me mad. I shared them with Sam, thought, and welcomed his mostly silent support. I shared them with my dad too even though I wasn't sure he wanted to see them.

"Doesn't it get to you?" He asked me one Sunday after I shared an image with him.

I looked at him, taking in what he said. He hadn't realized it wasn't because of my work that I was surrounded by death. *We all are.* I just chose to acknowledge it through my work. It was my way of keeping Keely present, visible, tangible. *It is my healing.*

I saved the finished product for each family to be the first to see their image. I wanted to give them the moment I had when I backed up and saw my babies in tangible form. I worked through nights, flipped the images upside down and sideways. I looked from every angle. I tucked easter eggs of deer and moose in, depending on the families' desires and their stories.

I looked at the noses and eye shapes of each sibling. I combined coloring and body types. I tucked in little bits of who they might have been. I had one single chance to do this right. I had dreams about these children I never met but felt like I knew them.

In the years it took to finish, one of the mothers, a friend of mine, had gone on to be with her daughter. I lamented that she never saw her image. It turned out that she was the only mother that was part of the images. She was part of it before she died. *It was just meant to be that way.*

I prepared for the opening and then we had to readjust. A worldwide pandemic took over our lives, our grief, and our art gallery openings. We adjusted for the county's requirements and just felt lucky we got to have an opening at all.

I tossed and turned the night before like I was in labor. *Had I done everything I could to perfect those images?* I had such a strong sense of Keely's face and demeanor – *what if I got the other children wrong?* I laid awake in prayer. Sometimes I make a deal with God to just pray myself to sleep. Many nights, it's the only thing that works.

Despite their requests to take a "sneak peek" —the nineteen families I photographed did not see their final pictures until that night. I wanted to make sure they were perfect before I put them into the world. I wanted to make sure their cheeks were rounded the way they might have been, their smiles curled like a sibling, or their hair feathered in a breeze just right. I didn't want a peek to ruin the moment I got to have with my picture — the emotional moment of *there they are.*

I adjusted my emotions when one of the first people through the gallery asked which was my family. She asked how old my child was when she died. When I told her, she looked me straight in the eye and said, "Are any of these not like yours, but a *real* loss?" I just stared back, not saying a word. Part of me wanted to see if she'd figure it out on her own. Would she realize how hurtful her words were? You could hear a pin drop. She continued "You know, like a *child*, not a baby."

It didn't make any sense to me, but I stood there considering if she loved her children less the younger they were. I don't get to tell her how to grieve, even how to grieve my child. Her passive attitude towards my daughter's life didn't take any spark out of my light — I wouldn't let it. But I didn't have the energy that day to tell her how her words stung. I channeled my energy into the families that trusted me with their precious children and the single image they'd have of their children all together.

Because of the pandemic, many families couldn't be there. Others made the trip, despite the danger of it shutting down at the last second. For the families that couldn't be there, we gave them their moment via video calls. Each time, as the mothers and fathers saw the faces of their children that I had built, my heart sunk into my stomach, and I held my breath. I'll never really know how each family felt, but I prayed it was enough for them. *As close to enough as I could offer.*

Each time I showed the family their image, I stepped away to allow them privacy. I felt like I shouldn't be there. I was showered in hugs and gratitude. I will carry each of those children and their stories with me always. It was my most important collection.

Throughout the opening, the words of the Bible rang through my mind. 1 Timothy 1:4 (KJV) reads "Greatly desiring to see you, being mindful of your tears, that I may be filled with joy."

We spent the opening filled with the bittersweet joys of seeing our children's faces, but it only could happen once.

***

Time whittles down those willing to sit with you for as long as it takes. The long-term response to grief becomes the people who have shared in a similar loss and, on a very limited basis, those compassionate souls who have been willing to put their hand on your shoulder to support you for the long haul. Those few people who have stayed to listen, to hear, have looked beyond their own experiences and made a tremendous difference in my grief.

Each of them has given me the goal of being more like them, more compassionate, more ready to listen, more ready to see past differences and find latent similarities. Like the Starbucks barista, who offered care and concern when she didn't have to. Or like my mom to the old man on the porch. These people are the unsung heroes that make meeting strangers hopeful — carrying a quiet legacy of compassion that lightens a stranger's load.

I continued creating artwork and photographs that told my biography of grief. I created an image to represent everyone wanting to grow old, but not realizing they'll often do that alone. I wasn't sure I'd find someone willing to be in that one. Within minutes of posting to social media, a friend contacted me asking if I'd like to use her dad. I warned them of the heavy subject matter, and they were still on board.

The old man's laugh lit up the room. We only met for 20 minutes or so. The image would be a composite so there was no perfecting it in the studio. A few different angles photographed, and he was off to see his sister in Alabama "for the last time".

"I'm so sorry." I replied and continued "Is she ill?"

"Oh no" he said with a laugh. "We're old!" His eyes lit up like a child at his joke.

"But you could have 20 more years!" I responded.

"I sure hope not. I have to get back to the Mrs." he said, referring to his wife who had passed fourteen years prior.

He filled the studio with his youthful light and was thrilled to have his modeling debut in his 80s. He never got to see his image — he passed away unexpectedly just before his image was public. *Every death is unexpected, really.*

He didn't get to see his image, but it has traveled the world telling a little part of his story. My friend didn't get to see her image with her two children together, but the image carries her legacy. Their legacy. Each legacy is a million words in a single image.

The more art I produced telling the story of bereavement — the more people have opened up to me about their own stories. Maybe wearing it on my sleeve allowed other people to share more readily. Maybe it is just the one thing most everyone has in common. Maybe the courage we've siphoned off our grief lays the foundation for who we become afterwards — the person others will remember after we're gone.

I've had the honor of photographing many souls just before they leave this earth and others yet just as they arrive. Each intricate relationship threading itself through the next. My perspective on grief has evolved through each loss and through the maturity of life in general.

Grief is just love in a different form. We all turn out to be the person saying the wrong thing at the wrong time *sometimes.* We all find the right words for the right person once in a while.

When we walk away from a conversation —we don't know which of those we were in those moments. We will all be on the receiving end of someone saying the wrong thing. Then we have to decide how that will shape us. Will we end up gracious or bitter? *Maybe a little of both, if I'm being honest.*

When I found myself searching for words to comfort a close friend's mother upon his passing — I found none. She had lost her husband and both of her sons to death far too young. Her son was like a brother to both Sam and me. He was in our wedding. His heart was so big and his love for people even bigger. In the more than 20 years we'd known him, loving people was what he did best.

He made mistakes — just like we all do. He answered for his sooner than expected. Strangers often focus on *how* someone dies, even when the reason why doesn't say anything about how he or she lived.

I looked his mother in the eyes at the funeral and found no words. I thought I might be better at this by 40. *With each loss —we all start over.*

I have spent most of my grief not having answers. Keely's death had no logical reason that we or doctors could find. Her death was a lightning strike. My mother's cancer diagnosis came without her fitting the description of who that cancer would come for. It didn't make sense. *More lightning.*

Though the lack of logic makes anger a normal response — whatever normal is —I had none. I seemed to find comfort in the fact these occurrences were like lightning strikes. I wasn't angry at God. I wasn't angry at the doctors. I wasn't angry, period. *Afterall — you can't control lightning.*

But after my friend died, it was logical. It was a culmination of choices he made that ultimately cost him his life. He made those choices under the influence, of drugs, of other people, of his grief. It was the logic that made me mad now. I wasn't angry at God. I wasn't angry at my friend. I was just angry. *Maybe logic wasn't all that helpful.*

Now, when I'm in a crowd of people, whether I'm at a funeral or in a mall, I see all these drowning people. They're all drowning for different reasons and in different ways, but at the bottom of the waterfall. I cannot change what brought them under the water.

When you see someone drowning in grief, try to override the response to change how they're doing it. Swallow any feelings that their grief makes you uncomfortable. Reach out your hand or, better yet, jump down there with them so they know they aren't alone. Maybe their eyes are too blurry to see you. You have to let them know you are there.

Whenever I see someone I used to know, I am clouded by what they did or didn't do. I ran into my best friend from childhood at a holiday fair with my sisters. It had been a couple of years since my mother died. She was with her mother. I had seen her occasionally as an adult just by happenstance.

But in childhood, we were constants in each other's lives. We signed birthday cards LYLAS for "love ya like a sister". We jumped on trampolines at midnight slumber parties and made Ouija boards out of notebook paper.

Our mothers planned every school party together and chaperoned every field trip. They *knew* each other. When she came up to hug me, of all the thoughts that swirled through my brain, and I could only focus on "she wasn't there" or "she didn't say anything" and "she didn't acknowledge".

Every word of our conversation during our brief encounter was muddled by anticipation that she would say something or remember — but she didn't. If she hadn't been there with her mother, maybe I could have focused on something else more. *I guess we'll never know.*

I have learned to try to let those things go. To let go of the footprints in the snow at the cemetery leading to only one headstone in the row of three. *Not everyone who grieves for my mother will grieve for my daughter.* Not everyone I want to remember her, or think will remember her, will do so.

My greatest fear of Keely being forgotten will not be realized while I'm alive. Beyond that — I have to let it go. My hope for her is beyond this earth.

Keely's death felt like I was weighted to the bottom of the ocean with cinder blocks holding me down. I was never able to push them off, but I grew stronger to carry them. They are still heavy, but I learned how to move with them. I'm used to them now — but it doesn't make them any lighter. I learned I can't let the low point of today determine the highpoint of tomorrow. *I have to start over every single day.*

I've learned the highlights we enjoy won't last forever. The golden hour starts fading just as it peaks — for us and for others. Soak in those golden rays of joy while they last and clap for others during their moments of bliss. *Theirs won't last forever either.*

I'm grateful for those who've sailed alongside me. Beyond disagreements and deep differences, I am little parts of everyone I've encountered. There are a lot of people who like to say they've sailed with you. But they're on a different boat. They'll wave across the ocean and be so proud you've sailed together. They'll take pictures as you careen off a waterfall and tell people how brave you were. They know because they were right there. They leave out that they didn't reach out to you. They certainly didn't follow you down to see how you were or offer help. But they sailed with you. So they say.

When you're at the bottom of that waterfall, the people you are there with are the ones who took the same route. You're all down there for a reason. The trip may have been different for each of you, but you all ended up in the same rough waters. Make sure to take someone's hand.

Now every visit to the beach is a visit with my mom. I let my feet sink into the sand and my senses take in all there is to offer. I have slowly started to find peace over sadness on those visits. I remember all of our trips as a child, as an adult, and all the trips we thought we'd have. Despite the great plans we made on the balcony over the beachfront pool that night, we didn't get all my parents' grandkids to the ocean together. Mom missed their 50th wedding anniversary by a matter of months.

We'll all end up at the bottom of the waterfall sooner or later. Take the pictures, take the day off, take in the moments that you'll have someday to cherish only as memories. I have lamented all the things I never thought to ask my mother and all the little moments we'll miss with Keely. *Would she like her toast cut into squares or triangles? I can't know.*

But maybe that's the beauty of life too – maybe those little secrets the dead take with them are a compilation of memories which make them uniquely special. It's not so much knowing those little moments — but loving the person that formed from them.

I continue to focus my energy on what I can do, what I can say, and who I can help. I lean into God and work my emotions out with pixels and oil paints. I have gathered up all the pieces of my broken heart and molded them into a sculpture that I hope brings someone peace.

I think the most important art comes from the biggest heartbreak. I know the most important healing comes from art, and I know that all the comfort and peace come from God. All good things do.

Occasionally, I get to be the vehicle for that healing in someone else. We're all remembered as entirely different people depending on who is doing the remembering. We've all been the hero and the villain in someone else's story. We've all found the wrong ways to grieve and the healing ways to remember. I've found my most comfortable path at the intersection of art and faith. I call on God to offer me ways to transform my emotions into a new creation; a portrait, a painting, a story without words.

I am still drowning. I don't have a choice in that, but at some point, down the road of grief —we get to decide how to drown. We can drown into baptism. We can drown in pixels and paints. We can drown into Christ.

We can drown in something more than we were before. There are many right ways to drown. These are mine.

Acknowledgements

First of all, words cannot express my gratitude for the amount of time, energy, love, and heart that my editor, Stephanie Miller, put into this work. Part editor, part therapist, she helped me sort through the whys time and time again. I am so thankful.

Thank you to my cat Zuzu Bailey for sitting on my legs in particularly stressful times – my own personal purring cat-weighted blanket, and to my geriatric puggle Braverman, for keeping me humble and never letting me forget I'm on deck for cleaning up his accidents.

A big thank you to my college professor and advisor, Deborah Hagedorn. During my first semester of college, I went to her to change my major from fine arts to political science. She refused, saying that if art was going to lose me to politics, I'd have to find someone else to do it. I didn't, and I am forever thankful.

Major thank you to all the brothers and sisters in Christ who have been a hand on my back whether they realize it or not. Throughout all the congregations we've been members of- Chicago, Evansville, Bloomington, Waco, I look forward to the prayers, hymns, growth, and fellowship.

About the Author

Aly Elliott currently lives in Indiana with her husband Sam and their five living children (Boston, Callum, Beckham, Marnie, and August), among the living memory of their daughter Keely. As a family, they travel the country and the world, taking in every sunset humanly possible. Aly is a portrait photographer and exhibition artist with work in 29 countries worldwide. She has undergraduate degrees in Fine Arts and Marketing, in addition to CPP, Master of Photography, Craftsman, and Master Artist degrees from the Professional Photographers of America. In 2024, she enjoyed the honor of earning first place in the Children and Teens category at the International Photographic Competition for an image titled "Troupe of One". She is also a speaker, focusing on business for artists and visual storytelling.

If you see someone furiously sketching ideas into a red notebook, you'll know its her.

www.ingramcontent.com/pod-product-compliance
Lightning Source LLC
Chambersburg PA
CBHW031456160726
47994CB00005B/2067